Secret Admirer: Behind the Curtains of a Parasocial Relationship

Samantha Jafar, Celina Lee, Anjali Singh, Nikita Chugh, Valerie Chow, Muhammad Ansar , Madison Coutinho

Secret Admirer: Behind the Curtains of a Parasocial Relationship

Samantha Jafar, Celina Lee, Anjali Singh, Nikita Chugh, Valerie Chow, Muhammad Ansar , Madison Coutinho

With Austin & Catherine Mardon

Design by Dana Mah

PRESS

Cover Design and Typesetting by Dana Mah
Additional design edits by Clare Dalton

Print ISBN 978-1-77369-853-3
E-book ISBN 978-1-77369-854-0

Golden Meteorite Press
103 11919 82 St NW
Edmonton, AB T5B 2W3
www.goldenmeteoritepress.com

Contents

Defining an Extrordinary Bond

By Samantha Jafar

Introduction

As soon as we are born, we form bonds with individuals. Humans are defined as social creatures that are highly interactive with other members of its species, and this in turn involves creating social links. Typically, this consists of familial relationships, love relations, friendships, acquaintances, work relationships, and many more. They generally involve more than one person where each cultivates their bond in various manners. An exception to this definition of a relationship is the concept of parasocial relationship. What is a parasocial relationship and what makes it so different from other relationships that humans form? The key difference is that there is only one person that provides the basis of this unique bond. A parasocial relationship is a one-sided relation where one party is unaware of the other. Surprisingly, this phenomenon has been long present in history although it's been only recently defined. Its history and origin, its present state, the causes and effects and its evolution in the future will be discussed in later chapters of this book.

So, What are We?

One of the issues of defining the relationship shared between a known personality and a fan is that the relation is unidirectional (Preiss, R. W. et al., 2006, p.301). There is an ambiguity in defining parasocial relationship and parasocial interaction. A normal relationship includes both parties developing their bond, but this is not the case in a parasocial relationship. Even if a celebrity sends a response to his fans, their bond isn't similar to the ones we normally cultivate in our daily lives. A fan may feel that they know the celebrity in an intimate manner, but that is not the case for the other party, especially if they have a large fanbase.

According to the Oxford Reference, the concept was coined by anthropologist Donald Horton and socialist R. Richard Wohl in 1956, where they referred to it as "a kind of psychological relationship experienced by members of an audience in their mediated encounters with certain performers in the mass media, particularly on television. Regular viewers come to feel that they know familiar television personalities almost as friends". As the number of contacts with the performer increases, the more we are likely to view the performer in an empathic manner and feel that they might know and understand us. Certainly, it can be observed that a person may dedicate emotional energy, time and interest towards the other party which often is a known figure. This individual is not aware of the existence of the viewer (Horton, Donald, & R. Richard Wohl. 1956).

The topics of parasocial relationships and interactions are very common between organizations (e.g., sports, spirituality and more), or are celebrities, artists, or television stars. The relation overcomes the social network in a manner that excludes the chances of being rejected. The viewer is likely to admire and choose to follow and identify with the individual of their choosing. Some may enter this bond due to the relief that there is no reciprocation or obligation for the other party as there is no real contact between themselves and the persona.

Solving the Ambiguity
As for the meaning of parasocial interactions, this involves the feeling of what an individual may experience when consuming a piece of media from an artist. For example, a person may feel that they belong in a friend group while watching a show involving a friend group (e.g., the show Friends). Indeed, certain shows adopt a setting that creates the illusion of familiarity for the viewers. Talk shows illustrate this fact by their setting which often involves a couch with the host always directly addressing the audience. Even if the relationship is one sided, many of the audience may feel that there is an intimacy with the performer on their screen. The term "parasocial interaction" is described as "a one-sided mediated form of social interaction between the audience and media characters. In doing so, they assume PSI [parasocial interaction] to be similar to face-to-face interactions between two individuals except that PSI [parasocial interaction] lacks mutuality while real social interactions feature bidirectional communication." (Liebers, N., & Schramm, H., 2019, p.2-5).

In addition, the interaction only takes place between the fan and the celebrity during media reception. Solving the issue of ambiguity, Parasocial relationship breaks this boundary by creating cross-situational relationships between the audience and media characters. Another difference between both terms is that parasocial relationships can tolerate single responses from the persona which can still develop into a relationship between a viewer and a performer. To clarify, a relationship can still take place even if the other party doesn't respond due to the fact that the fan accepts and tolerates the absence of such response. An interaction isn't possible as it needs another individual's response to the previous person's action.

Social Media-A New Horizon
 Though this definition of describing parasocial relationships and interactions persisted for several years, the introduction of a new media form that we now consume in our daily lives known as "social media" has drastically changed how we define a parasocial relationship. The relationship is not a real intrapersonal link that is formed by the constant contact of a fan and any content they consume where the celebrity is exposed. As the amount of contact increases, the more the brain perceives this contact as a face-to-face interpersonal contact rather than a single sided one. Having its origins in psychology and communication, the number of studies on parasocial relationships and interaction has increased thanks to the introduction of social media and its impact on the development of these particular kinds of relations.

Some argue that it is not the amount of contact that forms the bond, but rather, the quality that is received from the relationship. The manner in which one enters a parasocial relationship is not similar to how one is introduced to intrapersonal friendships in their life. Indeed, a parasocial relationship is often voluntarily entered, provides companionship, and it stems from social attractiveness (Preiss, R. W. et al., 2006, p.302). Most of the media content that helped in forming these bonds used to be found in television. The introduction of the Internet in the early 1990s was a major factor that favored and contributed to an increase of parasocial relationships. It is now possible for it to occur in settings such as blogs, video games or social media applications. The intimacy and the essence of parasocial interactions have evolved as well. The introduction of reality TV shows allows the viewers to have a closer glimpse into the lives of their favorite celebrity and the issues they face on a daily basis. By exposing the performer's struggles, a common trope in reality shows that capitalizes on human emotional vulnerability, which therefore make viewers feel more connected to the performers. In addition, media performers can also share their opinions and their thoughts on social media applications such as Twitter and Instagram which can be accessed by millions of users throughout the world. It is through these avenues that the audience discovers whether their favorite actor or musician shares the same values or preferences as them, whether that be their political standpoints or the brands they support.

When an actor performs a specific role such as the role of a parent in a family (e.g., the Adams Family), an individual in a friend group (e.g., Friends,), someone trying to get into or is already in a romantic relationship (e.g., Sex in the City) or just an employee in their workplace (e.g., Grey's Anatomy), we are able to perceive traces of a personality that we appreciate and relate to within these characters. Hence, this creates the basis for a parasocial relationship as the audience is able to develop a bond with the interactions of the character they perceive in the media.

Although, there is a difference in the formation of a parasocial relation when it involves a celebrity from a reality show, a musician or an actor that portray characters in comedies or drama, the fan creates a link with a human performer as they are deemed as real, while with a fictional character the audience are aware that the individual is not real which doesn't create a strong bond. There is a basis when it involves the actor that performs in fictional stories portrayed in movies. They are aware that the actor is real and that it can contribute to a strong parasocial relationship. This can be illustrated by the wide fan base for actors that have played superheroes or villains in the Marvel Universe. Indeed, the relationship can be deeper due to the fact that by being a real person, the audience believes that there is a chance they could interact with the celebrity in real life (Preiss, R. W. et al., 2006, p.302).

A Special One-Sided Bond

There are several causes that can contribute to the formation of parasocial relationships such as an individual may feel lonely and may want to look for ways to fill that lack of social interaction due to their shyness or fear of the public. It may also be out of pure pleasure where the celebrity is a contributor that furthers their interest (e.g., boybands such as BTS or One Direction). Whatever reasons it may be, they all support the unidirectional aspect of the bond shared between the involved individuals. The causes of parasocial relationships will further on be analyzed in later chapters. In addition, agency and consent is one of the elements that is largely present in this concept. In some intrapersonal cases such as family, the individual did not have the choice to be in that bond. It was something that was decided from the moment they were born in which they also didn't give consent to.

However, in this case, the audience has the choice to enter or leave the parasocial relationship depending on the choices of the persona. For example, a fan may stop supporting an artist if they find out that they don't share the same values anymore or if they found a flaw in a celebrity's actions. There is no effort given by the other party involved in this bond, which again justifies the notion of unidirectionality. The efforts provided by the audience depends on the set of expected values and standards they place on the artist which they compare their actual personality and actions to. The beginning and the end of this type of relationship is less complicated compared to intrapersonal relationships. It can also be less difficult emotionally as there is only one individual that is invested in the bond. If the character was fictional, the pain of separation may be different compared to the pain we would feel towards someone real. Another end to the relationship may be when a TV character dies on screen. Researchers have named this occurrence as a parasocial break up. All three terms are related and described as under the notion of parasocial phenomena shared between the audience and the media performer (Liebers, N., & Schramm, H., 2019, p.2-5).

Even if it is a one-sided bond, there are many similarities between traditional relations and parasocial relations where companionship is given on a voluntary basis. It supports the fact it is a relationship despite its unique nature. In fact, the individual may feel loyalty, positive emotions and feelings, and express gratitude towards the celebrity. They keep up with their news and whereabouts on the Internet, similarly to how we take news of friends and relatives in a different manner. It can also provide relief and support just like how we'd find in any intrapersonal relations. Some may view this type of relationship as a falsehood, but a parasocial bond can be as fulfilling as any other relationships for a human being.

Conclusion

To summarize, the concept of parasocial relationships involves that one party in the bond is not aware of the existence of the other. It often involves a bond between a viewer and a famous known personality and it frequently occurs in media content such as television or the Internet. Parasocial interactions are defined as one-sided interactions between an audience member and performer. The difference between both terms is that parasocial relationships involve a long-term aspect where one party gives consent to the nature of their relationship and still develops it. In the past, these bonds used to mostly happen with TV shows or books, but now it can also appear with blogs, social media applications or video games. Due to this, the nature of the relationship has also matured where the audience is in a more intimate contact with the performer. A unique aspect that can occur from these bonds is that it can create communities that are dedicated towards a persona, which normally wouldn't be found or created from interpersonal bonds.

References

Horton, Donald, and R. Richard Wohl. 1956. "Mass Communication and Para-Social Interaction: Observations on Intimacy at a Distance." Psychiatry (Washington, D.C.) 19 (3): 215–29. https://doi.org/10.1080/00332747.1956.11023049.

Liebers, N., & Schramm, H. (2019). Parasocial Interactions and Relationships with Media Characters – An Inventory of 60 Years of Research. Communication Research Trends, 38(2), 4–31.

Parasocial Interaction. Oxford Reference. Retrieved 1 Jul. 2022, from https://www.oxfordreference.com/view/10.1093/oi/authority.20110803100305809.

Preiss, R.W., Gayle, B.M., Burrell, N., & Allen, M. (Eds.). (2006). Mass Media Effects Research: Advances Through Meta-Analysis (1st ed.). Routledge. https://doi-org.proxy3.library.mcgill.ca/10.4324/9780203823453.

A Look Into the Creation of the "Star"

By Celina Lee

1920s Hollywood: Where Stars Began

Before the 1920s saw major reforms in Hollywood, eventually establishing the Classical Hollywood System, the industry followed the guidelines imposed by the MPPC (or the Motion Picture Parents Company), which was also known under the name the "Trust," (Cook, 1985, p.4). This group sought to provide some stability and consistency to a rapidly growing industry, but the strict rules imposed by the MPPC eventually led to its disbandment in 1915 after having been investigated by the Court in 1912 (Cook, 1985). Until this time, the MPPC was the sole distributor and exhibitor of films, requiring producers and exhibitors to "pay licensing fees to the Trust in order to purchase their patented equipment - for projectors, cameras, and raw film stock,"(Cook, 1985). This effectively prevented members of the organisation from "experimenting with new modes of production, distribution or exhibition," which was one of the major factors leading to the dissolution of the group (Cook, 1985). After 1915, new companies had formed, now experimenting with longer films and the use of stars as product differentiation between studios (Cook, 1985).

The year 1913 became a landmark year for changes within the film industry affecting every sector, from distribution, (to) exhibition (to) production (Keil, 2009). Public interest shifted towards feature films and multi-reels, as opposed to short films or actualitiés, which were popular from the 1890s to the 1910s (Keil, 2009). This was the beginning of the need for creativity to be streamlined as a form of labour (Regev, 2016). Hollywood productions now had to create a "unique organisation of the workforce, one that ensured both steady profits and creative innovation," (Regev, 2016). In a way, creativity was converted into industrial labour in a system where producers and directors were put in charge of an "assembly line" of creators all working towards the common goal of producing a certain film, before moving on to the next (Regev, 2016).

The shift to feature-length narrative films brought on the creation of the star and the star system. In fact, before the year 1907, there was no such thing as a film actor, since acting on screen was not yet considered acting because of the photographic nature of film at the time (deCordova & Gledhill, 1991). The term actor would have been reserved for stage acting, which interestingly already considered some of their players "stars, "(deCordova & Gledhill, 1991). . Instead, film actors were described as "posing," due to the difference in understanding the "photographic and theatrical conception of the body, between posing and acting," (deCordova & Gledhill, 1991, p.20).

The changes in production and types of films produced after 1907 largely impacted/influenced the way people acted in films, now focusing on narratives, instead of short documentary films (deCordova & Gledhill, 1991). As studios sought to reach broad audiences encompassing multiple social classes, it became imperative that films contained "both action and acting," as a way to appeal to this new audience (deCordova & Gledhill, 1991, p.23).

Then, the concept of product differentiation emerged through the "picture personality," whose creation is tied to the year 1909 and the "star," which emerged after 1914, although the former marked the beginning of the star system (deCordova & Gledhill, 1991). This excerpt by Keil summarises the new use of these groups of people as product differentiation (2009):

For several years (before 1913), many of the major film companies have made a practice of publicising their actors' names, and now, credit titles commonly appear within films. But in this year (1913), studios raise the importance of stars in the promotion of films to an unprecedented level, through advertising campaigns, contests in magazines, the sale of novelty items bearing the likeness of stars, and the coordination of personal appearances, interviews, and profiles. (p.95)

The picture personality worked under the name given to them by fans or their own legal names but their names were often omitted from discourse about them (however this was not entirely true as many manufacturers of magazines and such consistently revealed the names of their actors) (deCordova & Gledhill, 1991). In fact, names were kept in (semi) secrecy due to the public's difficulty with separating the actor's role onscreen to their real-life persona, or from their other roles they had previously taken (deCordova & Gledhill, 1991). Contrastingly, the star was someone whose life was publicised, allowing the public to have intimate knowledge of their private and public life (deCordova & Gledhill, 1991). Between 1909 and 1914, audiences learned to differentiate film from reality and began questioning the lives of actors beyond the screen (deCordova & Gledhill, 1991). The star's roles in films and their persona could now be separated, giving birth to a new type of relationship between the stars and the public (deCordova & Gledhill, 1991). Dyer writes the following to explain the creation of the "star" (2004):

Stars are involved in making themselves into commodities; they are both labour and the thing that labour produces. They do not produce themselves alone. We can distinguish two logically separate stages. First, the person is a body, a psychology, a set of skills that have to be mined and worked up into a star image. This work, of fashioning the star out of raw material of the person, varies in the degree to which it respects what artists sometimes refer to as the inherent qualities of the material; make-up, coiffure, clothing, dieting and body-building can all make more or less of the body features they start with, and personality is no less malleable, skills no less learnable. (p.5)

<u>Answered: Your Most Burning Questions About Your Favourite Star</u>

By the late 1920s, fan mails became a very prominent form of fan-star interaction. For example, actress Clara Bow was "receiving over 30,000 pieces of fan mail in one month," during this period of time (Barbas, 2000, p.211). Interestingly, at the time, fans and anything asked or written by them was highly controversial among members of studio teams (Barbas, 2000). Fan letters are an example of something considered a "nuisance," by studios (Barbas, 2000). These pieces often straddled the line between absurdity and sometimes, downright insanity. According to a list of requests compiled in 1939, letters contained the following requests from actors: "cigarette butts, shoes, chewed pieces of gum, a "blade of grass from star's lawn," and locks of hair, in addition to the usual demand for autographs and photos," (Barbas, 2000, p.205). However, the sentiment towards fans was different for those at the receiving end of this passionate love, stars understood that this community was vital to their longevity (Barbas, 2000). When a star's popularity somewhat came to a halt, in turn making a studio doubt their appeal playing lead roles, they turned to their legion of fans, creating a kind of "transaction" between the two parties where goods would be sent to fans who put a star back on the map (Barbas, 2000). Moreover, stars understood that their fans were the reason for their survival in the cutthroat industry, which meant that treating them with the utmost positivity was essential (Barbas, 2000).

Film studios obviously understood this as well, in 1928 alone, "Hollywood studios received over 32,250,000 fan letters and spent nearly two million dollars on postage, photographs, and salaries for the fan mail departments. But alienating fans would have been far more costly," (Barbas, 2000, p.208). Studios and their heads believed in the importance of fan letters as a barometer for a star's popularity or anything that had to do with whatever picture they might have appeared in (Barbas, 2000). For example, David O. Selznick (producer of Gone With The Wind, 1939) regularly perused fan mail to gauge fans' opinions on a wide range of issues, ranging from casting suggestions to the hiring of people of colour in predominantly white films (Barbas, 2000).

Fan magazines were incredibly popular during the 1920s, placing them in a similar element of fan culture as fan mail. At the time, fan magazines "existed not only to promote films but also to promote stars," and "these [fan magazines], which arguably exerted as much influence on the formation of star personas as much the films in which stars appeared, publicised and defined stars not only as screen performers but also as physical culture authorities," (Addison, 2002, p.17). These pieces of fan culture were mainly composed of the following elements: a question and answer section dedicated to a certain star, fashion advice, comments on a star's health regiment (from the star themselves) and popularity polls, among other things (deCordova & Gledhill, 1991).

One thing to note is that "early fan magazines depended to a large extent on the pleasure the public took in knowing the players' names," (deCordova & Gledhill, 1991). There seemed to be some degree of difficulty in the beginning of the history of the magazines in distinguishing the difference between the actor and the characters they may have played in various films (deCordova & Gledhill, 1991). This was especially evident in the question and answer sections of these publications. Before this new arrival in fan culture, there was no need to understand this intertextuality, as it only emerged when cinema had become prevalent enough for audience members to begin needing to differentiate their recognition of different "names" and their film appearances (deCordova & Gledhill, 1991).

Similarly to fan mail, fan magazines were used in market research conducted in order to gain more intimate knowledge on audience members (Stacey, 1991). However, these polls were hardly indicative of any meaningful qualitative data due to the nature of the polls, and their limited types of questions they could ask (Stacey, 1991). Typically, the questions were basic, seeking to deduce which stars were most popular during a certain period of time or asking moviegoers their reasoning as to choosing to see a particular film over another (Stacey, 1991). On the other hand, one component of the magazines that was considered more useful in determining the public's opinion on a star were the letter pages, as they were written by fans themselves and contained their "complaints, criticism, appreciation and likes and dislikes," (Stacey, 1991, p.148).

The power of fan mail and magazines held was phenomenal in the 1920s. Fan bases became impossible to ignore with the advent of the star system where audience members were interested in identifying themselves within the persona of a certain actor or the characters they may have played, something that emerged during this time with the creation of the new version of "acting." These groups were extremely passionate with the lives of their beloved stars, wanting to know them and their lives to an extreme degree, wielding a significant amount of power over their lives, and careers even.

Clara Bow. Occupation: It Girl

An example of a star under the star system in the 1920s is Clara Bow (1905-1965). Her tumultuous Hollywood career began in 1923, however it wasn't until the late 1920s that her fame skyrocketed, making her one of the most important figures working in the entertainment industry in her time (Orgeron, 2003). As a child, she had always been fascinated by films, especially since they were her only respite from her difficult school-life due to her stammering, and her home life due to abusive, self-destructive parents, (Stenn, 2000). As Bow put it, "In this lonesome time, when I wasn't much of nothin' and didn't have nobody, [there was] one place I could go and forget the misery of home and heartache of school. That was the motion pictures," (Stenn, 2000, p.12). As John Bennett, one of her friends recalled, "she told me that she was going to be a great movie star. Of course, I didn't believe her," (Stenn, 2000, p.13).

Interestingly, Bow's career began with her participation in a magazine contest, Motion Picture's: "Fame and Fortune" context (Orgeron, 2003). As previously stated, these pieces of literature were a way for audiences to become entangled in the stars' lives, ultimately creating "a concrete existence for themselves in relation to the star system," and "magazines were part of the mechanism of fandom out of a spectatorial demand for information," (Orgeron, 2003, p.79). Consumerism was one of the direct results of this effect, as readers (women in particular) were often advertised to by their favourite stars advertising products they (supposedly) endorsed (Orgeron, 2003). This became especially important as a large percentage of Bow's fandom were women at a time where women were slowly entering the workforce, essentially changing society's view on the place of the woman in society, as this population now had a newfound purchasing power (Orgeron, 2003).

According to Orgeron (2003), women were particularly drawn to the contests magazines offered as a way to "become actively involved with movie culture and in the process, to negotiate their own identities beyond the realm of their day-to-day experiences," (p.79)

Later on, Clara Bow was dubbed the "It Girl" of the generation. This nickname was derived from her role as a leading actor in the film It (1927) about a salegirl's (Betty Lou, played by Bow) romantic pursuit of the new owner (Cyrus Waltham, played by Antonio Moreno) of the department store where she works (Orgeron, 2003). Marsha Ogeron writes the following in an explanation regarding Bow's 1927 film It and its relationship to fan culture (2003):

Clara Bow's film It can be understood as a parable about fan culture, particularly the ways that fan magazines constructed female readers and Hollywood films positioned female spectators. It is replete with the interplay between plenitude and lack, with the elemental bases of spectatorial identification, and with the processes of personal reevaluation that were central to the machinations of female fandoms in the 1920s. Like fan culture, which encouraged women to imagine and, on occasion, to act out, certain fantasies about their identities in relation to star culture. It enacts a fantastic narrative of female sexual aggression and class transcendance. (p.82)

Essentially, the film catered to both the female and male gaze, setting itself apart from films released during this time that would have only focused on the male gaze. The film allowed its female star to become a participant and not only a passive passenger in the objectification happening in the film, acting as a sort of statement against "traditional modes of passivity," (Orgeron, 2003, p.83). This led to female spectators in particular to identify themselves onscreen through the character of Betty Lou.

In It, Betty Lou (Clara Bow) is an assertive character who is financially independent, chases her dreams and romantically pursues a man whom she fancies. These are all things that would have mirrored the desires of women at the time (or a percentage of women, at least) and for Betty Lou to enact this made her unique. Her sexual aggressiveness, which was conveyed through the use of skillful camera work and shot set-ups was particulalry revolutionary, even though changes in attitude towards female sexuality had been slowly progressing in the 1920s (Orgeron, 2003). The character of Betty Lou fulfilled the fantasies of female spectators, leading audience members to identify with her, validating their wishes, desires and their belonging in Bow's fandom (Orgeron, 2003).

Clara Bow is an interesting figure to examine through the lens of the early celebrity, as she is inevitably tied to the themes of consumerism, gender and fandom culture. None of these things can be separated from her, as this intertextuality is at the core of her existence as a star, as a thing to be consumed and loved. The beginnings of fandom and the parasocial relationship that blossoms from this culture can be observed in the life of Bow, providing a glimpse into the beginnings of such phenomena.

References

Addison, H. (2002). Capitalizing Their Charms: Cinema Stars and Physical Culture in the 1920s. The Velvet Light Trap, 50(50), 17. https://www.proquest.com/docview/2054567/fulltextPDF/9D041A96FD864536PQ/1?accountid=14771.

Barbas, S. S. (2000). Movie Crazy: Stars, Fans and The Cult of Celebrity, 1910-1950 (thesis). Proquest Dissertations Publishing, Ann Arbor. https://www.proquest.com/docview/304589395/fulltextPDF/678768B125724AFDPQ/1?accountid=14771.

Cook, P. (Ed.). (1985). History of the Cinema: Introduction & The American Film Industry. In The Cinema Book (pp. 4–5). Introduction, BFI.

deCordova, R. (1991). The Emergence of The Star System in America. In C. Gledhill (Ed.), Stardom: Industry of Desire(p. 17-27). essay, Routledge. https://books-scholarsportal-info.myaccess.library.utoronto.ca/en/read?id=/ebooks/ebooks2/taylorandfrancis/2013-03-14/1/9780203400425#page=45.

Dyer, R. (2004). Introduction. In Heavenly Bodies: Film Stars and Society (2nd ed., pp. 5). Introduction, Routledge. https://www-taylorfrancis-com.myaccess.library.utoronto.ca/books/mono/10.4324/9780203605516/heavenly-bodies-richard-dyer.

Keil, C. (2009). 1913: Movies and the Beginning of a New Era. In C. Keil & B. Singer (Eds.), American Cinema of the 1910s: Themes and Variations (pp. 95–96). essay, Rutgers University Press. https://doi-org.myaccess.library.utoronto.ca/10.36019/9780813546544-007.

Orgeron, M. (2003). Making "It" in Hollywood: Clara Bow, Fandom, and Consumer Culture. Cinema Journal, 42(4), 77-89. http://muse.jhu.edu/journals/cinema_journal/v042/42.4orgeron.html.

Regev, R. (2016). Hollywood Works: How Creativity Became Labor in the Studio System. Enterprise & Society, 17(3), 591–595. https://doi.org/https://doi.org/10.1017/eso.2015.89.

Stacey, J. (1991). Feminie Fascinations: Forms of Identification in Star-Audience Relations. In C. Gledhill (Ed.), Stardom: Industry of Desire (p. 148). essay, Routledge. https://books-scholarsportal-info.myaccess.library.utoronto.ca/en/read?id=/ebooks/ebooks2/taylorandfrancis/2013-03-14/1/9780203400425#page=168.

Stenn, D. (2000). 2. In Clara Bow: Runnin' Wild (2nd ed., pp. 11–13). essay, Cooper Square Press. https://www.google.ca/books/edition/Clara_Bow/GmgyQaH-UPm8C?hl=en&gbpv=0.

A Look Into the Creation of the "Star"

Parasocial Relationships & Mental Health

By Anijali Singh

The curtain unfolds. Your favourite star steps into the spotlight and the performance begins. They carry out their production, scene by scene, line by line. But you see past the flashing lights, costumes, and make-up. You feel a connection, finding yourself suddenly overwhelmed by the aura of this talented figure before you. Inspired. They make you feel complete, and your self-esteem grows. A sense of purpose and fulfilment has been found within you. Applause emanates from the crowd while the curtains close. The star steps back into the dark, but their character leaves an everlasting mark on your mind.

These few sentences illustrate the early emotional stages of a parasocial relationship. When we, the vaguely-defined audience, peek behind the curtains, blurring the bilateral boundary, we build a one-sided relationship with simply a name. The concept itself seems contradictory to the nature of a human, humans who crave connection and long for love and comfort (Stever, 2016). Foundationally, healthy relationships are a staple of humanity on the strength of establishing a sense of belonging, safety, and comfort (Stever, 2016). This emotional amenity is essential to the mental well-being and development of all involved parties in a relationship (Stever, 2016). However, parasocial relationships factor out reciprocity, requiring minimal "effort, obligation, and responsibility" (Horton & Wohl, 1956, p.215). Therefore, the psychological explanation for parasocial relationships, currently a contentious topic, is of keen interest.

As previously mentioned, pioneering research by Horton & Wohl (1956) proposed that parasocial relationships emerge due to "repeated exposure to a media persona," after which individuals develop "a sense of intimacy, perceived friendship, and identification with the celebrity" (Chung & Cho, 2017, p.3).

In this digital age, we carry the key to the social network 24/7, and all it takes is the push of a button. Pixels illuminate your screen. A thousand colours flash before your eyes. Vivid characters from your social media feed paint a perfect image. A perfect life. Your interest in these colourful personas grows. The figure on your screen is now simply yours… and this cues your social perception and interaction, stirring the ingredients of a parasocial relationship recipe (Horton & Wohl, 1956).

A Positive Outlook
The Benefits of Parasocial Relationships on Mental Health
In our media-saturated society, we encounter hundreds of faces, voices, and personalities on a daily basis, making the parasocial phenomenon a trending topic in the younger generation (Stever, 2016). Historically, parasocial relationships were believed to be "pathological" and a symptom of "loneliness, isolation, and social anxiety" (Kowert & Daniel Jr., 2021, p.4). However, recent studies support otherwise, suggesting that most parasocial interactions are benign and improve several dimensions of human health (Hoffner & Bond, 2022).

As a model, parasocial relationships play a part in forming an identity, establishing self-morals, and a sense of autonomy in adolescents (Giles & Maltby, 2004; Gleason et al., 2017). Mental health and identity are closely linked in that a person's self-perception affects their sense of self-worth and the way in which they value themselves (Giles & Maltby, 2004). Therefore, any outlets that influence individuality, including social media, can positively or negatively impact an individual's ability to practise self-acceptance (Giles & Maltby, 2004). In particular, the absence of reciprocity can be an outlet for them to "experiment with various ways of being" and determine their own set of principles (Gleason et al., 2017). Further exploring identity, the study found that the emotional gravity of parasocial processes strongly correlates to the endorsement of certain personality attributes in adolescents (Gleason et al., 2017). The experiment results revealed that adolescents built parasocial relationships through a hierarchical or egalitarian lens. Some perceive media figures in an authorial or role model position. These individuals find agentic, successful celebrities appealing and aim to include these qualities in their developmental goals (Gleason et al., 2017). Contrarily, others may construct parasocial relationships in peer contexts, simulating an egalitarian fashion. They use the imaginary facet of parasocial relationships to grow their autonomy from parental direction. This emotional autonomy encourages self-motivation which, down the road, will translate into meaningful growth in personal, social, and professional settings (Giles & Maltby, 2004). These specific individuals were also more likely to view their favourite celebrities as mentors who externalise "attractiveness and wisdom" (Gleason et al., 2017). Naturally, these "mentors" impart a framework for adolescents to blossom into the people they will become (Gleason et al., 2017). Despite these differences in relationship styles, fundamentally, the relational construction of media figures can act as a positive factor in shaping identity among adolescents. This imaginary relationship paves the way for them to create healthy relationships with themselves, which will be further discussed in chapter 6.

From a clinical perspective on development, parasocial relationships may be related to attachment styles in early childhood. To demonstrate, a study by Rain & Mar (2021) exemplifies parasocial relationships as a coping mechanism for individuals with avoidant attachment, a type of insecure adult attachment style characterised by self-directed behaviour and unease with intimacy (The Attachment Project,

2020). From a young age, children who have been taught to be independent and "tough" are susceptible to developing avoidant attachment in later years. As adults, these individuals may conceal their insecurities with confidence, but behind their masks, they struggle with emotional or physical intimacy, transpiring into an inability to build healthy, long-lasting relationships (The Attachment Project, 2020).

With reference to personality and psychopathology, developmental research suggests that social bonds we form in childhood immensely influence the ones we make later in life (Rain & Mar, 2021). Specifically, a caregiver who provides emotional support and reliability establishes the foundation for secure attachments (The Attachment Project, 2020). This emotional closeness facilitates a sense of stability and vulnerability while instilling self-assurance and a promising perspective on life at large (The Attachment Project, 2020). Individuals who lack this connection growing up may fill this void by immersing themselves in fantasies and fiction, such as engaging in parasocial relationships (Rain & Mar, 2021). Essentially, they satisfy their need for intimacy by employing the social and interpersonal elements of narratives that are unaccompanied by the threat of rejection (Rain & Mar, 2021). Furthermore, people with avoidant attachment can sometimes identify with television characters who exhibit autonomy and independence; hence, they may try to embody these characteristics as a coping mechanism (Rain & Mar, 2021). Although parasocial relationships are imaginary, they may feel "psychologically real" and "personally meaningful," which explains the involvement of attachment styles (Giles & Maltby, 2004). As illustrated, the findings of this study can be broadly applied in helping individuals with atypical behaviours linked to attachment processes.

Too Much Time and it Takes Over Your Mind
Dangers of Parasocial Relationships
Although the positive effects of parasocial relationships are well corroborated, not all of these relationships are entirely innocent. In fact, they may induce negative ramifications on development starting from early childhood. Specifically, when an element of fantasy materialises, reciprocal relationships are liable to be replaced with "on-screen" celebrities. This effect instigates a vicious cycle of maladaptive escapism. Although the corresponding behaviours displayed for relational maintenance may vary among individuals, the fabrication and commitment to a long-term imaginary companionship itself pose several risks to mental health.

Primarily, the invasion and subsequent substitution of a real-life relationship with parasocial relationships is an area of concern. Chandola et al. (2007) demonstrated that lack of reciprocity in "partnership, parent-children, and general trusting relationships" correlates to poorer mental and physical health. It may lead to anxiety, loneliness, and social isolation and more severely, contribute to depression (Chandola et al., 2007). Hence, the unilateral nature of parasocial relationships may become unfulfilling, and eventually a diversion from reality (Chandola et al., 2007).

Giles & Maltby (2004) corroborate these results, proposing that celebrities can exist as a "secondary group of pseudo-friends" for adolescents. They further explain that it becomes difficult to transition to reality if the adolescent intensely centralises on a single celebrity (Giles & Maltby, 2004). One such extreme case was John Hinckley Jr. — a name associated with the attempted assassination of US President Reagan.

Case Study: John Hinckley Jr. and an Attempted Assassination

On March 30, 1981, outside Washington Hilton Hotel, President Reagan was speaking to a union gathering when suddenly several shots were fired. John Hinckley Jr., gun in hand, shot the President and his entourage.

Tracing back, Hinckley had a virtually typical childhood. He was a good student and enjoyed sports but after moving and starting high school, his behaviour took a turn as he lost interest in his hobbies (Biography.com Editors, 2017). He spent the majority of his time alone, locked in his room, causing his social life to diminish (Biography.com Editors, 2017). Around the mid-1970s, Hinckley attended Texas Tech University, which he later quit. He then moved to California with the aspiration of pursuing songwriting (Biography.com Editors, 2017). During this time, he was beguiled by the film Taxi Driver, re-watching it over 15 times (Biography.com Editors, 2017). This 1976 film centers around a troubled, lonely New York cab driver fixated on "saving the world" by conspiring an assassination and rescue of a young prostitute, played by Jodie Foster. His interest in the movie evolved into an infatuation with Foster, and so in 1979, he purchased his first gun (Biography.com Editors, 2017).

In the following years, his psychological state was unsteady, causing a dramatic shift in his demeanour (Biography.com Editors, 2017). At this time, he started consuming antidepressants and sedatives and wrote to his sister "My nervous system is shot", followed by "I take heavy medication for it which doesn't seem to do any good" (Biography.com Editors, 2017). Evidently, he was struggling with a type of psychosomatic disorder as his words spur speculation on whether he entered the early phases of substance addiction.

In 1980, he decided to move back home and received some psychiatric treatment (Biography.com Editors, 2017). Unfortunately, the treatment was not effective in improving his symptoms or condition and he spiralled in the opposite direction. His enthrallment with Foster was still persevering, and this is when Hinckley began searching for ways to contact her. He finally called her, but she affronted his strange advances and rejected his attempts to make a connection (Biography.com Editors, 2017).

Regrettably, the story takes a dark turn when Hinckley believes his only way to win Foster's affection is by devising a dangerous scheme: to kill a president. His initial target was President Jimmy Carter, but he never executed this plan (Biography.com Editors, 2017). The target then fell to the next person on his agenda—President Ronald Reagan. Hinckley's justification was that his act of violence was an "unprecedented demonstration of love", drawing a comparison between his relationship with Foster to Romeo and Juliet (Biography.com Editors, 2017). Hinckley was arrested for several charges including attempting to kill the President and tried the following year (Alperstein, 2016). He was found not guilty by reason of insanity and was sent to St. Elizabeths Hospital, spending 35 years at this psychiatry facility (Alperstein, 2016).

John Hinckley Jr. was a man who was tired of the world around him and sought refuge in a different world, a world of fiction, away from his own. He was haunted by a shadow that ceased to exist, a shadow he created. It followed him everywhere, always on his mind. Imagination or reality? He couldn't see the line. He was labelled crazy, but his obsession was his only crime.

While Hinckley's story is not exemplary of a typical parasocial relationship, it portrayed the dangers of a prolonged, unchecked one. His actions were motivated by his imaginary relationship with media figure Jodie Foster, for whom he went to extraordinary lengths to impress (Alperstein, 2016). Hinckley's situation was categorised as pathological, but such parasocial interaction is not uncommon (Alperstein, 2016).

An Obsession is Born — Celebrity Worship Syndrome

Celebrity worship is a phenomenon that has gained significant popularity since social media increased interaction between audiences and public figures. While any individual in the public eye is susceptible to being an object of obsession, most research in the field suggests that television, film, and music stars are more likely to be targeted (Griffiths, 2013). Celebrity worship is an abnormal type of parasocial relationship, characterised by a monopolising and addictive nature, thus influencing clinical sequelae (Maltby et al., 2003). This topic is further explored in chapter 4, but in a psychogenic context, celebrity worship syndrome is an obsessive disorder in which an individual becomes excessively occupied with the details of a celebrity's private life (Griffiths, 2013). It often starts off as thinking you know the person on your screen a little more intimately.

You know their last name. You put it next to your first name.
You know their birthday. You mark it on your calendar.
You know their ex-relationships, and you wonder how someone could lose such a chance.
You know their favourite song. You put it on repeat.

You know their favourite style. You spend hours copying it.
You know their aspirations. You wish it was you.
You think you know someone, so you wholeheartedly believe you do.
A few moments with this figure on-screen vanquishes all your worries, if only fleetingly.
You invest so much time in their lives, watching, listening, waiting, but only pleadingly.
A little too much time… and it takes over your mind.

And just like that, an obsession is born. The series of acts, perhaps innocent individually, gradually piece together to form an obsession stemming from the roots of a parasocial relationship.

This syndrome directly affects extreme sets of attitudes and behaviours affecting personality as per Eysenck's theory (Maltby et al., 2003). Eysenck's theory claims that biological predispositions towards specific personality traits integrated with conditioning and socialisation during childhood create our personality (McLeod, 2021). Maltby et al. (2003) worked to relate personality traits as described in Eysenck's theory to the three dimensions of celebrity worship:

1. The entertainment-social dimension involves individuals who find celebrities' ability to entertain and be a social focus appealing (Griffiths, 2013)
2. The intense-personal dimensions concern individuals who exhibit intensive and compulsive feelings about a celebrity (Griffiths, 2013).
3. The borderline-pathological dimension describes individuals who display uncontrollable behaviours and fantasies about a celebrity (Griffiths, 2013).

Maltby et al. (2003) then demonstrated:
-People who worshipped celebrities for entertainment-social reasons may reflect extraversion and optimistic personality traits (Maltby et al., 2003)
-Intense-personal attitudes toward celebrities may reflect neuroticism traits such as emotional instability, anxiety, and solitude (Griffiths, 2013; Maltby et al., 2003)
-Celebrity worship of a borderline-pathological nature may reflect psychoticism traits (ex. aggression, impulsivity, and antisociality), indicating susceptibility to psychopathic disorders (Griffiths, 2013; Maltby et al., 2003)

Evidently, celebrity worship for a reason beyond entertainment is problematic, instigating unfavourable personality traits which may severely impact psychological integrity and health. Maltby et al. (2005) also suggested that most celebrity-obsessed individuals often face "high levels of dissociation and fantasy-proneness" (Griffiths, 2013; Maltby et al., 2005). While the Maltby et al. (2003) study was conducted on university student and adult sample sizes, they also investigated the impact of celebrity worship on negative body image in female adolescents aged 14-16. Intense-personal celebrity worship of actresses perceived as having a desirable body shape and size adversely influences body image in female adolescents (Maltby et al., 2005).

As a further illustration, in the Gleason et al. (2017) study, no female participants stated an athlete as their favourite celebrity. Sadly, this outcome is unsurprising. With the underrepresentation of female athletics in the media coupled with the impossible beauty standards of on-screen actresses, girls often face emotional pressures to be someone they think they need to be. As such, greater salience of athletes will allow young women to connect with celebrities exemplifying healthy body images and habits, ultimately fostering multifaceted development through the scope of mental and physical health (Gleason et al., 2017).

A Crafty Illusion

Conclusion on the Effect of Parasocial Relationships on the Mind

Conclusively, parasocial relationships are closely intertwined with mental health and development. The parasocial process is an illusion. A crafty illusion that impersonates parts of a real-life relationship, manipulating a sense of intimacy, friendship, and identification. With the inevitable invasion of social media in our personal lives, and recently, the rise of a participatory culture in media, the mutual line between performer and spectator is being erased (Alperstein, 2016).

From an evolutionary perspective, humans look up to those who receive attention from society, which would have been elders or good hunters in prehistoric times (Griffiths, 2013). But in the modern era, these respected individuals are actors, television stars, musicians, and micro-celebrities, whose fame and fortune make them entities of emulation (Griffiths, 2013).

While this connection has many benefits in shaping identity and development in the younger generation, there are equally important risks when these public figures replace our real-life friends. Intense emotional investment in a fictional world is when we question the consequences of parasocial relationships. This illusion recklessly plays with the strings of mental well-being, so we must draw back the curtains with vigilance, for it is not a person that awaits us but rather an abstraction of the mind.

References

Alperstein, N. (2016, July 29). John Hinckley, Jr. and a Tale of the Current Political System. Medium. https://medium.com/@NeilAlperstein/john-hickley-jr-and-a-tale-of-the-current-political-system-4dc212ce4fe9.

Biography.com Editors. (2017, April 27). John Hinckley Jr. - Reagan, Assassination & Facts - Biography. bio. Biography.com. https://www.biography.com/crime-figure/john-hinckley-jr.

Chandola, T., Marmot, M., & Siegrist, J. (2007, October). Failed reciprocity in close social relationships and health: Findings from the Whitehall II study. Science Direct, 63(4), 403-411. https://doi.org/10.1016/j.jpsychores.2007.07.012.

Chung, S., & Cho, H. (2017, April). Fostering Parasocial Relationships with Celebrities on Social Media: Implications for Celebrity Endorsement. Psychology & Marketing, 34(4), 481-495. https://doi.org/10.1002/mar.21001

Giles, D. C., & Maltby, J. (2004, March). The role of media figures in adolescent development: relations between autonomy, attachment, and interest in celebrities. Science Direct, 36(4), 813-822. https://www.sciencedirect.com/science/article/abs/pii/S0191886903001545.

Gleason, T. R., Theran, S. A., & Newberg, E. M. (2017, February 23). Parasocial Interactions and Relationships in Early Adolescence. Frontiers in Psychology, 8. https://doi.org/10.3389/fpsyg.2017.00255.

Griffiths, M. (2013, July 5). Celebrity Worship Syndrome. Psychology Today. https://www.psychologytoday.com/ca/blog/in-excess/201307/celebrity-worship-syndrome

Hoffner, C. A., & Bond, B. J. (2022, June). Parasocial relationships, social media, & well-being. Science Direct, 45. https://doi.org/10.1016/j.copsyc.2022.101306.

Horton, D., & Wohl, R. R. (1956). Mass Communication and Para-Social Interaction. Psychiatry, 19(3), 215-229. 10.1080/00332747.1956.11023049.

Kowert, R., & Daniel Jr., E. (2021). The one-and-a-half sided parasocial relationship: The curious case of live streaming. Science Direct, 4. https://doi.org/10.1016/j.chbr.2021.100150.

Maltby, J., Giles, D. C., Barber, L., & McCutcheon, L. E. (2005, February). Intense-personal celebrity worship and body image: Evidence of a link among female adolescents. The British Psychological Society, 10(1), 17-32. https://doi.org/10.1348/135910704X15257.

Maltby, J., Houran, J., & McCutcheon, L. E. (2003, January). A clinical interpretation of attitudes and behaviours associated with celebrity worship. The Journal of Nervous and Mental Disease, 191(1), 25-29. 10.1097/00005053-200301000-00005.

McLeod, S. (2021). Theories of Personality. Simply Psychology. https://www.simplypsychology.org/personality-theories.html.

Rain, M., & Mar, R. A. (n.d.). Adult attachment and engagement with fictional characters. Journal of social and personal relationships, 38(9), 2792-2813. https://doi.org/10.1177/02654075211018513.

Stever, G. S. (2016, March). Evolutionary Theory and Reactions to Mass Media: Understanding Parasocial Attachment. Research Gate, 6(2). 10.1037/ppm0000116.

The Power Dynamics in a Parasocial Relationship and their Use and Abuse

By Nikita Chugh

Trigger warning: Sexual assault, grooming, child abuse, stalking, violence
Exhausted from his concert, he sank down into his couch with a sigh. Just another day being the most loved person in Hollywood, he thought. It didn't give him the same thrill, the same excitement that he used to feel years ago. Oh well, he thought, it still had its perks. Picking up his phone, he scrolled through the profiles of the thousands of fan Instagram DMs he had received. He clicked on one of the girls' profiles, and read, Age:16, Lives in Los Angeles. Perfect, he thought with a smirk. He replied to her message with an invitation to add him on Snapchat. She, of course, instantly replied, gushing over him and thanking him. He smiled, and thought gleefully, Hook, Line and Sinker. Little did he know, she was staring at him through his open window right outside of his living room.

Through the Lens of Fame
Power in the hands of the Media Figure
A huge power dynamic exists between a celebrity, with high social status, wealth, and influence, and a fan. The term "influencer," quite literally describes this unique dynamic where the media figure has the power to influence their followers. Having a parasocial relationship further enhances the danger of this power imbalance, because the fan usually does not recognize the celebrity as posing a threat to them. They are often blinded by trust and admiration, and it is this vulnerability that media figures can take advantage of. With allegations that have surfaced across the internet against social media influencers such as Shane Dawson, James Charles, and Tony Lopez, it is important to understand how fans, especially minors, are at risk of being cybergroomed or taken advantage of by popular media figures.

In a parasocial relationship, underaged fans are at particular risk of being manipulated and cybergroomed by influencers that they look up to. When content creators make interpersonal content with high levels of relatability and entertainment value towards a younger audience, the strength of the parasocial relationship increases (Conner, 2021). Thus under the influence of this relationship, underaged fans, when confronted with direct online or in-person contact with a media figure, may feel like they are under pressure to engage in certain acts, for example, sexual ones.

Cybergroomers often exploit victims by using their need for attention and validation, along with their low self-esteem, and personal issues, which is a reason why adolescents are most affected disproportionately (Wachs et al., 2012). They are at the greatest risk of being the target of cybergrooming, compared to younger children, presumably also because of their increased usage of anonymous chat platforms, as well as lack of monitoring from an adult figure (Livingstone et al., 2018). Adolescents are also more receptive to sexual explorative conversation and exchange with strangers, as well as are more likely to engage in risky online behaviour (Wachs et al., 2016). This includes sending nude or semi-nude pictures over social media as a response to the instigator online, often to prove commitment and maturity (Wachs et al., 2015).

Case study: James Charles
Information from- Vulture article titled: "A Timeline of James Charles Allegations and Controversies," by Florence O'Connor and Zoe Haylock.

James Charles, a popular Youtuber, vlogger and famous make-up artist, has been known for the allegations and accusations of being sexually explicit with minors. Charles often employs several strategies in his videos in order to seem more relatable and closer to his fans, who he calls "sisters". Some of these include talking about his personal issues to his fans, vlogging his life as though bringing viewers alongside him, and using humour that will appeal to his target audience, which mostly consists of younger teens.

It all started in February 2021, when 4 underaged boys, previously his fans, first alleged that Charles groomed them and pressured them to exchange sexual images over social media platforms. Some of them shared screenshots of their sexually charged conversations, and one claimed that James continued to flirt with him even after learning of his age. Charles responded to these accusations over Twitter, claiming that he was not aware of the boys' ages during the interaction. In March of that same year, another 15-year-old boy came out against Charles, equipped with screenshots and the sexually explicit photos they had exchanged, claiming that James was also fully aware of his age at the time of their conversation.

James Charles then posted a video on Youtube, talking about these allegations, and providing justification for his actions. He admitted that he was desperate, and unaware of the power imbalance between celebrity and fan. "What I wasn't getting before is that the excitement that comes from talking to a celebrity is literally enough to make somebody do or say something they normally wouldn't, even if that celebrity isn't intentionally weaponizing their fame, money, or power," Charles said. After this video, many others continued to come out with their own stories of their sexually negative experiences with James Charles, which he denied and threatened legal action.

Analysis: This example highlights how minors may often be manipulated by powerful figures that they admire and look up to. Fans who are underaged are at greater risk of being groomed by those they have developed a strong parasocial relationship with, because of their lack of full comprehension of the situation, and the danger they may be putting themselves in. James Charles had done an excellent job cultivating a relationship between himself and his fans, which may have led to his fans feeling close to him, and being obligated to be sexual when he asked, despite it making them potentially uncomfortable. James Charles himself acknowledged this effect, as seen by his quote from his video, and yet accusations against him continued after his promise to do better.

A Twisted Level of Devotion
Power in the hands of the fan

Celebrity worship syndrome, as mentioned before, is defined through an obsessive behaviour pattern, when a fan becomes excessively involved in a celebrity or media figure's life. This often involves knowing and tracking intimate details about them through a variety of sources, and even tracking their location at times (Meloy et al., 2008). We have seen celebrities talk to their fans over different types of social media in familiar and understanding tones, so as to develop a stronger perceived relationship with them. A portion of the fans who may be psychotic, may misinterpret this tone to mean something more than what the celebrity intended (Wilson et al., 2018).

There is also a possibility of dissociation, which causes one to have detachment from normal reasoning, and reality, as well as disintegration over control of acceptable thoughts, feelings and emotions (Maltby et al., 2006). People who dissociate may begin to fantasise things like "If celebrity X just got to meet and know me, they will definitely fall in love with me." There are thinner or non-existent boundaries in this kind of parasocial relationship, completely justified in the mind of the worshipper. Individuals who worship celebrities to a higher extent feel as though they have different and unique insights into personal issues of a celebrity (McCutcheon et al., 2002). They develop a certain addiction and eventually a tolerance to the delusive and dissociative behaviour, as a search for their own identity (McCutcheon et al., 2002). Sometimes, these obsessions have the risk of angering them, when things do not go the way they planned. Such attachments and obsession also then carry the risk of becoming intrusive, leading to stalking, and attacking figures as a personal goal to become closer with that person, or seek revenge (Meloy et al., 2008).

Media figures and popular celebrities are naturally at a higher risk of being the object of obsession of pathologically obsessed people, due to their increased exposure to the public eye. For example, celebrities in a reality TV show will be at a comparatively higher risk than others to be a target of such an attachment, due to them revealing intimate details of their daily lives that would otherwise not be known.

Minor celebrities may be even more vulnerable to such attacks, due to their lower rates of possession of security and surveillance (Wilson et al., 2018). This creates another form of power imbalance in the parasocial relationship, one where the fan has the knowledge, means and ability to stalk, attack and harm the celebrity, and the celebrity is unaware of the fan's existence, much less their intentions. Many celebrity stalkers aim to find their life purpose and self-identification through these obsessions, through which stalking becomes a proactive fan behaviour that helps them achieve these goals. Another type of unwanted pursuit of intimacy has been termed "obsessive relational intrusion (ORI)," which is similar to stalking but does not cross the threshold to count as a threat (Spitzberg & Cupach, 2007). Most stalking behaviours begin with ORI, and may become stalking when the boundary into potential harmful behaviour or intrusion of privacy is crossed.

Several tactics are employed by the stalker in order to get closer and gain more access to the victim (Spitzberg & Cupach, 2007). Different surveillance measures may be employed without the victim's awareness to obtain more information about their activity and whereabouts, through covert means. Again, this is increasingly easier to do for media figures in the public spotlight, who often catalogue their day-to-day activities on social media, such as posting pictures, stories and sharing their location, so as to maintain a parasocial relationship with their fans. Next, the stalker may try to communicate with their victim through letters, emails, cards, graffiti, and other ways of contact often obtained through cyberstalking (Nadkarni & Grubin, 2000). Invasion tactics may also be employed, which could break legal boundaries. Such activities include trespassing on their property, breaking and entering, and sending threatening messages (Spitzberg & Cupach, 2007). Finally, violence, physical or sexual assault and aggressive behaviours may be employed towards the victim. Dissociative behaviours are associated with violence at times, which may explain why some obsessed fans can be dangerous towards celebrity victims. Sometimes, their target of violence cannot be reached, due to being closely guarded and protected. This may then lead to the fan displacing violence onto close friends or family of the intended victim (Wilson et al., 2018).

It is not only celebrities who fall victim to these volatile behaviours from fans, but anyone in the public eye who has parasocial relationships with their supporters, such as politicians. The results of a survey conducted in the UK revealed that 81% of members of the parliament had experienced behaviour related to stalking, and 18% had been subjected to an attack, or an attempted attack (Wilson et al., 2018). The frightening length at which these individuals go to, demonstrated after the murder of Rebecca Schaeffer, a famous actress and model in the USA in 1989, prompted an amendment to stalking laws within California, as well as the establishment of a Los Angeles Police Department Threat Management Unit (Wilson et al., 2018).

The necessity for education and awareness for celebrities with large or comparatively smaller public followings should be emphasised in order to protect people from these instances. The treatment of such underlying mental disorders that cause fans to become intrusive towards people they are parasocially involved with is also important, and if caught and intervened early, can prevent further psychosocial or physical harm to the victim.

Use my Code for 20% off!

The influence of digital celebrities on the purchase intentions of consumers
Celebrity endorsements have been used widely in order to advertise products or enhance the image of a brand by associating it with a popular media figure or influencer. Parasocial relationships also tend to have the power to influence or persuade the purchase intentions of the viewers of a media figure. The viewers or fans have low persuasion knowledge, and due to the illusion of reciprocity and a real relationship, they are more inclined to buy what is advertised by the figure (Breves et al., 2021). Think of when you are recommended a product by a close friend, versus when someone you are not familiar with gives you the same reviews. You would probably be more inclined to trust your friend's opinion, which you know is probably reliable.

Similarly, when followers reach an advanced stage of a parasocial relationship, with perceived trust and authenticity, they more blindly trust the media figure and are not affected even if the advertisement is explicitly disclosed (Breves et al., 2021). The entertainment value of influencers strengthens the parasocial bond between themselves and the viewers, and positively predicts their brand trust more than the informative content about the branded advertisement (Lou & Kim, 2019).

If the media figure communicates effectively and clearly about the brand or products in said advertisement, followers may see them as trustworthy sources of information, and may be further influenced to make impulsive purchases (Hwang & Zhang, 2018). Because of this reason, marketers often develop long-term relationships with digital celebrities, so the same idea can be reinforced into the followers' minds, leading to increased brand trust and credibility. When brands can create the media figures into brand evangelists, that is, someone who participates in the active and continued vocal and behavioural support of a brand, it leads to strong consumer networks based on the trust shared by viewers into their parasocial relationships (Hwang & Zhang, 2018).

Another aspect that affects the purchasing influence in a parasocial relationship is the consumers' self-esteem. Individuals with low self-esteem may use monetary purchases as a coping strategy to uplift their self-identity, even if they view the media figure advertising to have low credibility (Bi & Zhang, 2022). This is why social media and its influencers may also cause the formation of materialistic tendencies in adolescents. When influencers serve as a role model to this impressionable category of consumers, they can inadvertently encourage peer pressure and social comparisons among teens, this in turn drives the materialistic foundation for their views, and causes increased purchasing intentions (Lou & Kim, 2019). The driving motive for this could be improving themselves or their status among their peers who presumably also follow the said media figure.

A Vote for Me, A Voice for You
Parasocial relationships in terms of predicting political outcomes
The effects of parasocial relationships can also be seen extending into the political realm, from the strength of the parasocial relationship between the voter and the politician influencing voting outcomes. People who have formed a parasocial relationship with politicians feel as though they have a sense of closeness and intimacy with them, and seeing the politician give speeches or talk, they feel as though they themselves are being addressed personally (Tsfati et al., 2021). Political experts and media campaigns constantly try to use tactics to increase an emotional bond with the viewers, so as to create parasocial relationships and persuade voters (Full Article: Intimacy Appeals in Israeli Televised Political Advertising, 2008). Furthermore, the focus of news coverage has also experienced a move from information about the parties and views to the individual candidates and leaders. This personalisation makes figures more familiar, as if they knew the politicians' personal lives more than their professional ones (Tsfati et al., 2021). Parties focused on religion, especially, tend to have advertisements with emotion based appeals. Left wing parties also have been found to use more intimacy based appeals than right leaning parties (Full Article: Intimacy Appeals in Israeli Televised Political Advertising, 2008).

Another important point as to why politically based parasocial relationships are so easy to form and maintain is because politics is based in reality. Unlike some other examples where parasocial relationships are formed with characters in a TV show or a book, political figures seem more authentic and are able to relate to the voters' lives (Full Article: Intimacy Appeals in Israeli Televised Political Advertising, 2008). These techniques have prompted questions about the ethics of the "issue versus image" problem (Full Article: Intimacy Appeals in Israeli Televised Political Advertising, 2008). Based on a logical approach, voters must evaluate each candidate based on their platform and ideas rationally, considering whether they would benefit the voters and community at large. Some think that when voters are swayed by the emotional appeal of ads and parasocial relationships, the rational way of thinking is suppressed. This is especially dangerous when politicians are aware of this and use voters' emotional reactions to propagate their selfish political propaganda (Full Article: Intimacy Appeals in Israeli Televised Political Advertising, 2008).

Another interesting factor in political parasocial relationships is the type of political system in the country in question, as well as its democratic maturity. The strength of parasocial attachments has been found to be higher in presidential systems like those in Indonesia and the U.S.A, than in parliamentary systems, such as those found in New Zealand (Hakim & Liu, 2021). A reason for this is that separating the president from the legislative body, may enable the voters' to form a more intimate parasocial relationship with them (Hakim & Liu, 2021).

All in all, parasocial relationships extend beyond entertainment with celebrities or influencers, into political figures and decisions, which may affect entire countries' fates. Therefore, it is essential to understand how politicians use the media and their power to project desired images and cultivate an imaginary relationship with voters, in order to manipulate political outcomes.

References

Bi, N. C., & Zhang, R. (2022). "I will buy what my 'friend' recommends": The effects of parasocial relationships, influencer credibility and self-esteem on purchase intentions. Journal of Research in Interactive Marketing, ahead-of-print(ahead-of-print). https://doi.org/10.1108/JRIM-08-2021-0214.

Breves, P., Amrehn, J., Heidenreich, A., Liebers, N., & Schramm, H. (2021). Blind trust? The importance and interplay of parasocial relationships and advertising disclosures in explaining influencers' persuasive effects on their followers. International Journal of Advertising, 40(7), 1209–1229. https://doi.org/10.1080/026504 87.2021.1881237.

Conner, F. (2021). The Relationship Between Parasocial Relationships and Grooming as a Problematic Rhetorical Strategy on YouTube. 20.

Full article: Intimacy Appeals in Israeli Televised Political Advertising. (2008). https://www.tandfonline.com/doi/full/10.1080/10584600802197327?scroll=top &needAccess=true.

Hakim, M., & Liu, J. (2021). Development, Construct Validity, and Measurement Invariance of the Parasocial Relationship With Political Figures (PSR-P) Scale. International Perspectives in Psychology, 10, 13–24. https://doi.org/10.1027/2157-3891/a000002.

Hwang, K., & Zhang, Q. (2018). Influence of parasocial relationship between digital celebrities and their followers on followers' purchase and electronic word-of-mouth intentions, and persuasion knowledge. Computers in Human Behavior, 87, 155–173. https://doi.org/10.1016/j.chb.2018.05.029.

Livingstone, S., Mascheroni, G., & Staksrud, E. (2018). European research on children's internet use: Assessing the past and anticipating the future. New Media & Society, 20(3), 1103–1122. https://doi.org/10.1177/1461444816685930.

Lou, C., & Kim, H. K. (2019). Fancying the New Rich and Famous? Explicating the Roles of Influencer Content, Credibility, and Parental Mediation in Adolescents' Parasocial Relationship, Materialism, and Purchase Intentions. Frontiers in Psychology, 10. https://www.frontiersin.org/article/10.3389/fpsyg.2019.02567.

Maltby, J., Day, L., McCutcheon, L. E., Houran, J., & Ashe, D. (2006). Extreme celebrity worship, fantasy proneness and dissociation: Developing the measurement and understanding of celebrity worship within a clinical personality context. Personality and Individual Differences, 40(2), 273–283. https://doi.org/10.1016/j. paid.2005.07.004.

McCutcheon, L., Lange, R., & Houran, J. (2002). Conceptualization and measurement of celebrity worship. British Journal of Psychology (London, England : 1953), 93, 67–87. https://doi.org/10.1348/000712602162454.

Meloy, J. R., Sheridan, L., & Hoffmann, J. (2008). Stalking, Threatening, and Attacking Public Figures: A Psychological and Behavioral Analysis. Oxford University Press.

Nadkarni, R., & Grubin, D. (2000). Stalking: Why do people do it? BMJ : British Medical Journal, 320(7248), 1486–1487.

Spitzberg, B. H., & Cupach, W. R. (2007). The state of the art of stalking: Taking stock of the emerging literature. Aggression and Violent Behavior, 12(1), 64–86. https://doi.org/10.1016/j.avb.2006.05.001.

Tsfati, Y., Cohen, J., Dvir-Gvirsman, S., Tsuriel, K., Waismel-Manor, I., & Holbert, R. L. (2021). Political Para-Social Relationship as a Predictor of Voting Preferences in the Israeli 2019 Elections. Communication Research, 00936502211032822. https://doi.org/10.1177/00936502211032822.

Wachs, S., Jiskrova, G. K., Vazsonyi, A. T., Wolf, K. D., & Junger, M. (2016). A cross-national study of direct and indirect effects of cyberbullying on cybergrooming victimization via self-esteem. Psicología Educativa, 22(1), 61–70. https://doi.org/10.1016/j.pse.2016.01.00.

Wachs, S., Junger, M., & Sittichai, R. (2015). Traditional, Cyber and Combined Bullying Roles: Differences in Risky Online and Offline Activities. Societies, 5(1), 109–135. https://doi.org/10.3390/soc5010109.

Wachs, S., Wolf, K. D., & Pan, C.-C. (2012). Cybergrooming: Risk factors, coping strategies and associations with cyberbullying. Psicothema, 24(4), 628–633.

Wilson, S., Dempsey, C., Farnham, F., Manze, T., & Taylor, A. (2018). Stalking risks to celebrities and public figures. BJPsych Advances, 24(3), 152–160. https://doi.org/10.1192/bja.2017.22.

Fandoms and Parasocial Relationships: A Cycle That Never Ends

By Valerie Chow

Introduction

ARMY, Swifties, Potterheads, Whovians. You've probably seen these words used in passing on social media over the years, but maybe you don't know what they actually mean. These are examples of fandom names. Fandoms, short for Fan domains, are communities that are formed around various popular cultures. These fandoms are made up of, obviously, fans. While there are "enjoyers", referring to those who are simply enjoying a form of media or entertainment, fans that are members of a fandom are not only engaged in the media, but also with each other (Busse & Gray, 2011).

Come to the dark side, we have cookies!
The benefits of joining a fandom

Now, what is the point of a fandom, when you are capable of enjoying a piece of entertainment on your own? Being part of a fandom allows for group identification, which is defined by Henry et al. (1999) as "member identification with an interacting group and is distinguished conceptually from social identity, cohesion, and common fate". Group identification has been shown to positively affect health and well-being (Reysen et al., 2017). For example, fandoms can alleviate loneliness and enable safe interaction with others that share a similar passion. Oftentimes, fans may feel isolated from their other friends due to a lack of shared interest or may fear being judged or are ashamed of their passion. By joining a fandom, fans can interact with others without that fear and worry, as they know they have the same interests, and therefore, are able to make friends. Fandoms also offer a sense of community and belonging, and with social media, are easily accessible. This may explain why fandom names exist, such as the examples listed prior, as it allows fans to better locate and identify with the fandom.

When part of a fandom, fans will usually participate in fandom activities, which allows the fans to partake in escapism, or interact with other members within the fandom. Some examples of fandom activities include (O'Donovan, 2016): Talking about your interest on social media. This can be done either publicly, such as blogging or tweeting, or privately, such as in direct messages or personal conversations

Attending a convention, which allows fans to interact with other members of the fandom, in-person, and meet and possibly speak with celebrities

Cosplaying, in which a fan may wear and/or make outfits or do their hair and makeup to look similar to a fictional character or celebrity

Consuming or creating fan-made content based on the original work. Some examples would be fanfiction, in which fans may write a story surrounding their piece of media, fanart, in which fans create visual art surrounding their piece of media, and fanvids, in which fans create videos, like edits, animations, and analysis videos, surrounding their piece of media

Using fanspeak, which is a language that is developed and understood by members of a fandom

Shipping in which fans become interested and support two or more characters or celebrities in a romantic relationship, regardless of if this is the case in the source material

Fandom Activities x Parasocial Relationships

How fandom activities and parasocial relationships influence one another

Fandom activities and parasocial relationships go hand-in-hand, in which fandom activities can influence parasocial relationships, and parasocial relationships can influence participation in fandom activities. In a study by O'Donovan (2016), they found that fans that have increased intensity in their parasocial relationships, meaning they feel closer and more intimate with their parasocial figure, participate more in fandom activities. This could be due to fans becoming more willing to participate in discussions or wanting to continue to learn more about their media figure. It was also found that fandom activities also result in a fan feeling closer to their parasocial figure, which may be due to the availability of content, especially online. Easy online access allows fans to learn details and personal anecdotes of their parasocial figure more easily (O'Donovan, 2016). In addition, consuming and creating fan-made content, such as fanfiction, has also been seen to influence parasocial relationships. This may be because a fan consuming or creating fan-made content of a parasocial figure would provide opportunities to form emotional attachments, experience admiration or relatability for struggles and experiences within the story, and observe fictional intimate details (Rivkah, 2020).

As a result, the consistent exposure to fan-made content and frequent participation in fandom activities resulted in a stronger parasocial bond between the fan and the media figure.

In my personal opinion, I also believe that the fandom's normalisation of parasocial relationships and behaviours may also play a role in parasocial relationships. With the normalisation and acceptance of this type of fan behaviour, fans can then accept their feelings towards the matter and further explore their parasocial relationship. For example, a new fan may observe many other fans' participating in a parasocial relationship within the fandom, leading them to either believe this is the norm or another type of fandom activity and therefore, stumble into a parasocial relationship in hopes of "fitting in". The normalisation of parasocial relationships in fandom spaces also opens opportunities to discuss these topics, such as learning how to stay safe, preventing being taken advantage of, and ensuring that a parasocial relationship does not get too intimate or become unhealthy. As a result, a fan who may be just developing or has already developed a parasocial relationship can understand what they are feeling, and ensure that they can draw a line between themselves and their parasocial figure. However, this normalisation can also be seen as a negative, in which a fandom, or a vocal minority within a fandom, may set more harmful behaviours or unhealthy parasocial relationships as the norm, resulting in newer fans believing that this is an acceptable way to act as part of a fandom. I will now discuss examples of parasocial relationships and fandom culture, and their impact on the fan, the parasocial figure, and others.

Case Study: Live Streamers

Live streaming has been quickly growing, with the industry experiencing a 99% year-over-year growth of hours watched in 2020 (Butler, 2021). Live streamers can use a variety of different streaming platforms, such as Twitch, Youtube, or Facebook, to produce content in real-time. What makes streaming unique from other entertainment media, like TV shows or YouTube videos, is the ability for streamers to interact with their audience in real-time. As a result, streamers and their audience have a unique parasocial relationship in which the subject of the parasocial relationship appears to be interacting with the user. Kowert and Daniel (2021) explain that the relationships between a fan and the streamer introduce the potential for reciprocal communication through chatting or donations, the formation of a community through interactions with others during a live stream, and the presence of the streamer as a result of constant accessibility to the streamer, either through live streams or social media. In addition, streamers also have fandoms, in which the fans are loyal to the streamer without caring about the type of content they are producing (Kowert & Daniel, 2021). For example, someone may watch a live streamer to see someone play their favourite video game, but a person who is part of the streamer's fandom will watch the streamer despite the video game that is being played.

In my personal experience with streamers and their corresponding fandoms, I found that the fandoms play an important role in maintaining the parasocial relationship between a fan and a live streamer. It is quite easy to interact with the fandom itself since when the streamer goes live, a space is created to communicate with other members of the fandom via chat boxes. A live stream also allows fans to indirectly or directly interact with others in the fandom through a shared experience, such as reacting to the live stream, also known as live-blogging or live-tweeting. As a result, people within the fandom can bond over their shared enjoyment and admiration for a streamer simultaneously. When there is no live stream going on, participating in fandom activities is also common, and can consist of making fanart, reblogging/retweeting gifsets, creating clips, and more. Thus, the constant stream of fan-produced media ensures that the cycle of fandom interactions and the intensity of parasocial relationships continues without pause.

However, I have also observed that the fandom itself plays a role in ensuring a healthy parasocial relationship, done similarly to a mother teaching their child manners. For example, some live streamers have established "boundaries", which function similarly to a list of rules that the fandom should follow. In addition, the boundaries may act as a way to prevent the formation of unhealthy parasocial relationships. For example, some creators have asked not to say "I love you" with a romantic context, to not be referred to by their real name but rather, to be called by their online username, to not share private photos of the content creator, or to refrain from asking privacy-invading questions, such as questions regarding sexuality or relationship status (smp-boundaries, 2020). As a result, streamers are able to draw a clear line between themselves and their fans, as well as, show their dislike for fans who act against their boundaries, thereby preventing the development of unhealthy parasocial behaviours. Fans will typically ask the streamer themselves for their opinions on certain things, such as fan-made content or shipping, or the streamer will state boundaries themselves.

From my experiences, fans usually will respect the streamer's boundaries, as well as discourage those who act against them. In addition, these boundaries are commonly discussed or easily accessible through dedicated accounts on various social mediums, such as Tumblr and Twitter, allowing newer fans to quickly adapt, which may prevent the formation of unhealthy parasocial relationships. Thus, the collective fandom creates a space that allows a fan to continue their admiration, emotional engagement, and fandom activities while also respecting the streamer.

Case Study: Voltron: Legendary Defender
TW: Mentions of Doxxing, Death Threats, Physical Assault
In 2016, the first season of the animated series, Voltron: Legendary Defender, was released on Netflix. As a reboot of the Voltron franchise, it roughly followed the same plot: In a battle against a tyrannical empire that is trying to take over the universe, 5 space pilots from Earth - Shiro, Keith, Lance, Hunk, and Pidge - operate a lion robot that combines to form a robot warrior, "The Defender of the Universe, Voltron", the only weapon that can save the universe (Dos Santos et al., 2016-2018). Unlike its original, Voltron: Legendary Defender introduced a diverse cast, including Allura, who portrays a woman of colour, Shiro, a queer and disabled Japanese man, Hunk, a Samoan man, Pidge, who was a male in the original series but was changed to a female, and Lance, who is Cuban (Dos Santos et al., 2016-2018). With this diverse cast of characters, a fascinating sci-fi plot, and nostalgia, Voltron: Legendary Defender gained a large fanbase. However, as the series continued, releasing a total of 8 seasons by 2018, the Voltron: Legendary Defender fandom was known across the internet as one of the most toxic fandoms.

First, let's define what we mean by "toxic". The term is typically used when there is a hostile response toward a person or media (Williams & Bennett, 2021). While many Voltron: Legendary Defender fans were simply enjoying the show and partaking in different fandom activities, some fans adopted this toxic behaviour, which was seen through various methods of harassment, such as blackmail, doxxing, physical assault, and death threats, towards both other members of the fandom and to the cast and creators of the show. Now, why were these actions occurring? A dissertation written by Drouin found that the most significant motivation for this type of behaviour was shipping (Fans Are Going to See It Any Way They Want': The Rhetorics of the Voltron: Legendary Defender Fandom, 2021). One of the most popular ships within the fandom, as well as on the internet at the time, was "Klance", a romantic pairing being the characters Keith and Lance. This was the major ship within the fandom, though other pairings between different characters were also discussed. However, a vocal minority believed that Klance was the only ship that should occur, within the fandom and within the show itself. This escalated to targeted harassment towards other fans that did not support this relationship. When Allura and Lance had a romantic relationship within the show, and when the show ended without Klance becoming canon, the harassment and death threats turned towards the cast members and executive producers.

I believe this toxic behaviour may have also been a result of an unhealthy parasocial relationship that developed with Lance and/or Keith. These two characters were the most popular: Keith, with his struggles in identity and, undergoes character growth from a socially awkward, lone wolf to a great leader and friend, and Lance, who is portrayed as a go-lucky, but also an insecure and self-deprecating boy, and is experiencing homesickness and struggling for recognition (TheTopTens, n.d.). Many fans admired these characters and found them relatable, as many fans are people who are experiencing loneliness, struggling to make friends or feeling alienated from their current friends, or undergoing personal struggles and dilemmas in their life. As a result, fans enjoyed following Keith and Lance as they developed and grew past their flaws, as this allowed the fans themselves to grow as well by projecting themselves onto these characters. Thus, it only makes sense that a parasocial relationship would develop between these characters and the fans who watch them and that fans would wish for what they believe would be their character's happiness. However, as the show went on and we witness Keith and Lance's relationship grow and regress, coupled with the desire for queer representation within a show that had proved they could provide a diverse cast, fans became frustrated and obsessed with the development of this relationship, possibly leading to an unhealthy parasocial relationship.

With a large fandom and Klance being one of the largest pairings, ranked as the #1 ship in 2017 and 2018 on Tumblr (Fandom, 2017; Fandom, 2018), it was easy for this unhealthy parasocial relationship to continue to grow in intensity. Fandom activities, such as fanart, fanfiction, and character analysis, were posted on various social media daily. Thus, fans had a constant stream of new fan-made content to consume. This increased the intensity of the participation within the fandom, as well as made it difficult to step away from the fandom platform and its content. This may explain the intensity of the parasocial relationships these toxic fans experienced. In addition, the negative behaviour could then be explained as a result of a parasocial break-up. As discussed by Cohen (2004), parasocial breakups are more impactful depending on the intensity of the relationship. Thus, the fan's toxic response to seeing other fans reject their ship or the ship not becoming canon within the show could be perceived as a parasocial break-up and the denial of it. As the Voltron: Legendary Defender fandom became more known for its toxic behaviour and it was actively discussed within and outside the fandom, the unhealthy parasocial relationships and behaviours become normalised. As a result, younger fans who were joining a fandom for the first time may have believed this to be appropriate behaviour and acted on it. Thus, the fandom became a space that allowed/permitted this unhealthy parasocial relationship and behaviour to grow.

Additional Tags: Angst with Happy Ending
The progress fandoms have made
The normalisation of parasocial relationships within a fandom has its benefits and consequences. As parasocial relationships become more known, and are used as a marketing strategy or by the media figure, it is important that these discussions about parasocial relationships and how to handle them are occurring in fandom spaces. Over the past few years, we have seen the consequences of parasocial relationships, such as the grooming of younger fans by a media figure (as discussed in Chapter 4). We've also seen how fandoms are able to elevate these harmful behaviours, such as sending death threats (as seen in the Case Study: Voltron: Legendary Defender). Luckily, in part to this, fans who have seen these consequences occur are now more knowledgeable about the dangers of parasocial relationships and can spread that knowledge to newer fans. It isn't uncommon for fans who have been in many fandoms or older fans who have been part of fandom culture as a whole for some time to discuss parasocial relationships: to remind other fans that we don't really know a media figure, to warn younger fans of the power imbalance of parasocial relationships, to prevent fans from being taken advantage of due to their obsession, to advise fans to take a step back from the content and return to real life.

Conclusion
Being a part of a fandom provides many benefits, such as alleviating loneliness and providing a sense of belonging. Fandom activities and parasocial relationships can directly affect each other, causing participation in a fandom and the intensity of the parasocial relationship to increase. While there is a common belief that fandoms and parasocial relationships are dangerous and unhealthy, I believe that whether or not it is dangerous is dependent on the fans, and their acknowledgement and discussion of these types of behaviours. Recognizing what is appropriate

behaviour and acknowledging the danger and potential of parasocial relationships, fandoms can create a community that can develop into a healthy and safe space for fans to enjoy their shared passions.

References

Busse, K., & Gray, J. (2011). Fan Cultures and Fan Communities. The Handbook of Media Audiences, 425–443. https://doi.org/10.1002/9781444340525.ch21.

Butler, R. R. (2021, February 2). Going Live Online: The State Of Live Streaming And The Opportunities For Brands. Forbes. https://www.forbes.com/sites/forbesagencycouncil/2021/02/04/going-live-online-the-state-of-live-streaming-and-the-opportunities-for-brands/?sh=223345084b97.

Cohen, J. (2004). Parasocial Break-Up from Favorite Television Characters: The Role of Attachment Styles and Relationship Intensity. Journal of Social and Personal Relationships, 21(2), 187–202. https://doi.org/10.1177/0265407504041374.

Dos Santos, J., Montgomery, L., Koplar, T., Koplar, B., & Myung, Y. J. (Executive Producers). (2016-2018). Voltron: Legendary Defender [TV series]. Dreamworks Animation Television; World Events Production.

Fandom. (2017, December 4). 2017's Top Ships. Tumblr. https://fandom.tumblr.com/post/168182191859/tumblr2017-ships.

Fandom. (2018, November 28). 2018's Top Ships. Tumblr. https://fandom.tumblr.com/post/180587157919/2018-ships.

Fans are Going to See it Any Way They Want': The Rhetorics of the Voltron: Legendary Defender Fandom (Ph. D). (2021). Renee Ann Drouin. https://scholarworks.bgsu.edu/eng_diss/98/.

Henry, K. B., Arrow, H., & Carini, B. (1999). A Tripartite Model of Group Identification. Small Group Research, 30(5), 558–581. https://doi.org/10.1177/104649649903000504.

Kowert, R., & Daniel, E. (2021). The one-and-a-half sided parasocial relationship: The curious case of live streaming. Computers in Human Behavior Reports, 4, 100150. https://doi.org/10.1016/j.chbr.2021.100150.

O'Donovan, R. (2016). 'To boldly go where no psychologist has gone before": effects of participation in fandom activities on parasocial relationships. Journal of Applied Psychology and Social Science, 2(1), 41-61. https://ojs.cumbria.ac.uk/index.php/apass/article/view/298.

Reysen, S., Plante, C., & Chadborn, D. (2017). Better Together: Social Connections Mediate the Relationship Between Fandom and Well-Being. AASCIT Journal of Health, 4(6), 68-73.

Rivkah, G. (2020). Revisiting parasocial theory in fan studies: Pathological or (path)illogical?. Transformative Works and Cultures. https://doi.org/10.3983/twc.2020.1989.

smp-boundaries. (2020, February 26). SMP Creator Boundaries Masterpost. Tumblr. https://smp-boundaries.tumblr.com/post/611044520230109184/smp-creator-boundaries-masterpost.

TheTopTens. (n.d.). Top Ten Best Voltron: Legendary Defender Characters. https://www.thetoptens.com/voltron-legendary-defender-characters/.

Williams, R., & Bennett, L. (2021). Editorial: Fandom and Controversy. American Behavioral Scientist, 66(8), 1035–1043. https://doi.org/10.1177/00027642211042290.

Parasocial Relationships Influenced by Gender Indentity in Tweens and Adults

By Muhammad Ansar

How does the gender of an individual affect the formation of their own parasocial relationships?

As discussed earlier, parasocial relationships are one-sided, almost virtual relationships where an individual feels a strong bond or a connection with media characters or figures (eg: Youtubers, celebrities, fictional characters, sports teams etc). However, during the process of developing, fantasising or constructing these one-sided parasocial relationships, the individual rarely loses awareness of their own identity (Hall, 2020). It is crucial to note that the formation of these parasocial relationships has been on the rise due to the COVID-19 pandemic because of the increase in social media exposure due to social distancing protocols, online schooling and virtual workplaces (Bond, 2021). Furthermore, the increased reliance on screens as tools to online schooling and virtual workplaces has led to the strengthening of these parasocial relationships among individuals, as the lines between real-life (virtual) friendships and one-sided relationships with celebrities' have blurred (Bond, 2021). Because of the rise in parasocial relationships as well as the strengthening of these relationships due to the COVID-19 pandemic, it is important to study these relationships and the factors that influenced them. The implications of the COVID-19 pandemic on the development of parasocial relationships will be further discussed in Chapter 7.

One of the factors that has been shown to influence the construction of these parasocial relationships is the gender identity of an individual. For instance, gender schema theory, a theory in psychology developed by Sandra Bem in 1981, has suggested that children watch members of their own culture to learn appropriate vs inappropriate behaviour and values (Bem, 1981). This theory further states that children look up to members of their own gender to learn how to behave as either male or female (Bem, 1981). Additionally, according to this theory, once children are at an age where they have formed their own gender identity as a male or female (usually between the ages of nine and twelve), they begin to form mental conceptions of acceptable activities, norms, qualities and attributes of that gender (Bem, 1981). In other words, they begin to form mental conceptions of what is socially acceptable for them to do (or not do) as a male or a female.

Fact or Myth: Does the gender identity of an individual REALLY affect and influence the parasocial relationships they form?

Previous studies have shown that a child's gender affects their attachment to television and movie characters. Reeves and Greenberg (1977) provided a selection of well-known characters to children aged 8, 10, and 12 and asked them to score the figures on a variety of attributes. Results from this study showed that children of all three age groups gave same-sex characters higher ratings than those of the opposite sex (Reeves & Greenberg, 1977). In another study, Hoffner (1996) interviewed children between the ages of seven and twelve and asked them about their favourite TV character. After gathering data and running statistical analyses, she observed that nearly all the boys in the sample and about half of the girls selected TV characters who had the same gender identity as their own (Hoffner, 1996). In another paper with a sample of 370 middle schoolers (between the ages of ten and twelve), Steinke et al. (2006) found that boys and girls identified more with male and female scientist characters, respectively.

Tweens, between the ages of nine and twelve, are also at an interesting developmental stage in their life when it comes to gender identity development. At this time in their life, tweens usually step out of essentialist thinking associated with early childhood (ie: values and things that are important to their parents and families, rather than themselves) and begin to understand and adopt their very own ideas for gender (Halim and Ruble, 2010). There has also been a wide range of research that shows changes in brain development in tweens before and during adolescence, which may be associated with identity formation (with regards to gender). In scientific literature, the word "adolescence" is usually used to describe the time period in one's life where that individual transitions from childhood to adulthood (Arain et al., 2013). One of the brain changes that has been observed in tweens via longitudinal MRI studies is the (second) surge of neuronal growth that occurs right before puberty (Giedd et al., 1999; Baird et al., 1999). Neuronal growth refers to the growth of nerve cells or neurons that takes place in the brain to further accommodate cell function (and learning, memory and therefore, plasticity). This neuronal growth in tweens is evident through the thickening of grey matter and is very similar to the neuronal growth that is seen in infancy as part of neurogenesis (the formation of new neurons prenatally) (Giedd et al., 1999; Baird et al., 1999). Furthermore, research has shown that a second wave of synaptogenesis also occurs in the human brain during the adolescent years (Arain et al., 2013). Synaptogenesis refers to the formation of new, functional connections between neurons in the human brain which facilitates cell to cell communication as well as neuronal plasticity (ie: neuronal changes that occur in the acquisition of new skills that allows individuals to learn and adapt) (Giedd et al., 1999). Therefore, some of these changes in the human brain around adolescence may be linked with this gender identity formation that is seen in tweens.

Research by Martinez and Olsson (2019) has shown that tweens (aged nine through twelve years) use Youtube as a source of information and informal learning. This is significant because social learning theory in psychology states that children can learn new behaviours just by observing others and imitating them (Bandura, 1977). In other words, tweens can learn new behaviours by watching Youtube videos and imitating the values, lifestyles, behaviours and attributes of their favourite YouTubers. Oftentimes, the formation of these new behaviours goes hand in hand with the formation of parasocial relationships (with those YouTubers) among tweens. In addition, it has been noted that children often learn these new behaviours from role models that are highly attractive and most similar to themselves (Bandura, 2001). Therefore, it is safe to assume that similarity to oneself will most likely also play a significant part in the formation of these parasocial relationships.

Tweens select gender-congruent YouTubers to form parasocial relationships with According to gender schema theory, tween boys are more likely to seek out male YouTubers and form attachments to them compared to tween girls who are more likely to seek out and develop bonds with female YouTubers. However, these attachments and bonds usually tend to be one sided, which is why they can be referred to as "parasocial relationships". In a recent study with a sample size of 161 children between the ages of nine and twelve, Tolbert and Drogos (2019) found that tweens select gender-congruent YoutTubers as their favourite more often than they select YouTubers of a different gender. In order to eliminate gender bias, the male to female ratio in this study was 48% male and 52% female. To further prevent other types of biases, these children were recruited through several different means including schools, public libraries and university events in the Southern United States. The racial breakdown of the sample was as follows: 59% white, 23% mixed race, 6% Asian, 5% Hispanic, 4% Black, and 3% identified as "other" (Tolbert & Drogos, 2019)..

By conducting this study, Tolbert and Drogos (2019) examined the role of one's gender and how it can influence or affect the attachments and parasocial relationships that individual forms. The results from this study indicated that 97.2% of all tween boys (from the sample) selected a male YouTuber as their favourite. Similarly, 65.3% of all tween girls from the sample selected a female YouTuber as their favourite. Through these statistics, it is evident that the gender of the tweens (male vs female) affected who they developed a bond with (which can be indicative of the formation of parasocial relationships later on down the line). Even though 34.7% of all the girls did not select a female YouTuber as their favourite in this study, a post hoc test (a statistical test that is conducted after a result is found to be statistically significant, in order to determine where exactly that/those difference(s) came from) was conducted which showed that girls were significantly more likely to report a female YouTuber than a male YouTuber (Tolbert & Drogos, 2019). Therefore, this study shows tweens are more likely to form attachments (and therefore parasocial relationships) with YouTubers that are the same gender as themselves. Adults and young adults select movie characters whose actors have the same gender identity as them.

Another study by Hall (2020) set out to examine if participants are most likely to select a fictional movie character who is the same gender as them (in terms of the one they feel the closest to). Researchers collected and analysed data from one hundred and forty seven participants in two waves through surveys. The first survey was conducted in December 2017 when Marvel's Thor: Ragnarok and DC's Justice League had dropped and the second survey was conducted in March 2018 after Marvel's Black Panther and Star Wars: The Last Jedi came to theatres (Hall, 2020). Researchers ensured that people who had submitted the survey twice in both waves were excluded from analysis. The racial breakdown of the sample of participants in this study was as follows: 67% White, 23% Black, 2% Asian, 5% Hispanic and 3% identified as "other". A majority of the sample was made up of adults and young adults. To be specific, seventy-two percent of the total participants in this study were between the ages of 18 and 25 (Hall, 2020).

To evaluate the observed data, Hall (2020) carried out a chi-square analysis (a statistical test that results in a chi-square statistic which highlights the amount of difference that occurs between the observed and expected finding(s) within the sample) to figure out if the percentage of participants who selected a character of their own gender (as the one they felt the closest or most connected to) was different than what would be expected by chance. This chi-square analysis showed significant results ($p < 0.001$), providing support for the initial hypothesis that stated that participants are more likely to pick a fictional movie character who is the same gender as themselves as the one they feel the closest to. Because participants tended to feel the most connected with a fictional movie character that was the same gender as themselves, these participants are also more likely to form parasocial relationships with these same characters. Therefore, it is evident that the gender of an individual can influence or (affect) the parasocial relationships they form throughout their life.

Furthermore, similar to the Tolbert and Drogos (2019) study, some women in the Hall (2020) study were also more likely to select a male character as their favourite, compared to the men in the sample. For instance, 39% of the female participants in the Hall (2020) study selected a male character from these four movies as their favourite (compared to the 23% of men who selected a female character from these four movies as their favourite). However, this could just be because of the overrepresentation of male characters, YouTubers, and actors in global media compared to female representation. In this study, each of these four films featured a strong, well-liked, and positively portrayed female (Hall, 2020). However, two of these films, Thor: Ragnarok and Wonder Woman, only had one female character in them: Valkyrie (played by Tessa Thompson) and Wonder Woman (played by Gal Gadot), respectively. Because of the overrepresentation of male leads within these films (and the media in general), it serves as a likely possibility as to why 39% of the female participants in the Hall (2020) study selected a male fictional character as their favourite (and are thus, most likely to form parasocial relationships with). Therefore, to conclude, the gender identity of an individual does shape their attachments, bonds, and connections with others and also influences the parasocial relationships they form.

References

Arain, M., Haque, M., Johal, L., Mathur, P., Nel, W., Rais, A., Sandhu, R., & Sharma, S. (2013).
Maturation of the Adolescent Brain. Neuropsychiatric Disease and Treatment, 9, 449–461. https://doi.org/10.2147/NDT.S39776.
Baird, A. A., Gruber, S. A., Fein, D. A., Maas, L. C., Steingard, R. J., Renshaw, P. F., Cohen,
B.M., & Yurgelun-Todd, D. A. (1999). Functional magnetic resonance imaging of facial affect recognition in children and adolescents. Journal of the American Academy of Child and Adolescent Psychiatry, 38(2), 195–199. https://doi.org/10.1097/00004583-199902000-00019.
Bandura, A. (1977). Social Learning Theory. Englewood Cliffs, NJ: Prentice Hall.
Bandura, A. (2001). Social cognitive theory of mass communication. Media Psychol. 3,
265–299. https://doi.org/10.1207/s1532785xmep0303_03.
Bem, S. L. (1981). Gender schema theory: a cognitive account of sex typing. Psychol. Rev. 88, 354–364. https://doi.org/10.1037/0033-295X.88.4.354.
Bond, B. J. (2021). Parasocial relationships as functional social alternatives during pandemic-induced social distancing. Psychology of Popular Media. https://doi.org/10.1037/ppm0000364.
Giedd, J. N., Blumenthal, J., Jeffries, N. O., Castellanos, F. X., Liu, H., Zijdenbos, A., Paus, T.,
Evans, A. C., & Rapoport, J. L. (1999). Brain development during childhood and adolescence: a longitudinal MRI study. Nature neuroscience, 2(10), 861–863. https://doi.org/10.1038/13158.
Halim, M. L., and Ruble, D. (2010). "Gender identity and stereotyping in early and middle
childhood," in Handbook of Gender Research in Psychology, eds J. C. Chrisler, and D. R. McCreary, (New York, NY: Springer), 495–525. https://doi.org/10.1007/978-1-4419-1465-1_24.
Hall, A. E. (2020). Audience responses to diverse superheroes: The roles of gender and race in
forging connections with media characters in superhero franchise films. Psychology of Aesthetics, Creativity, and the Arts. https://doi.org/10.1037/aca0000363
Hoffner, C. (1996). Children's wishful identification and parasocial interaction with favorite
television characters. J. Broadcast. Electron. Media 40, 389-402. https://doi.org/10.1080/08838159609364360.
Martínez, C., and Olsson, T. (2019). Making sense of YouTubers: how swedish

children

construct and negotiate the YouTuber Misslisibell as a girl celebrity. J. Children Media

13, 36–52. https://doi.org/10.1080/17482798.2018.1517656.

Reeves, B., & Greenberg, B.S. (1977). Children's perceptions of television characters. Hum.

Commun. Res. 3, 113-127. https://doi.org/10.1111/j.1468-2958.1977.tb00510.x.

Steinke, J., Applegate, B., Lapinski, M., Ryan, L., & Long, M. (2006). Gender differences in

adolescents' wishful identification with scientist characters on television. Sci. Commun. 34, 163-199. https://doi.org/10.1177/1075547011410250.

Tolbert, A. N., & Drogos, K.L. (2019). Tweens' Wishful Identification and Parasocial

Relationships With YouTubers. Front. Psychol. https://doi.org/10.3389/fpsyg.2019.02781.

COVID-19's Impact on the Development of Parasocial Relationships

By Madison Coutinho

COVID-19 Implications

As we have discussed, humans are social creatures and need social interaction in order to lead healthy lives. Social interaction has been a huge part of human lives evolutionarily, and it is precisely these relationships that have enabled human beings to survive as long as we have. Forming relationships with other humans was crucial to early human survival. Humans banded together in social groups in order to forage, hunt, and for protection against predators, thereby increasing their chances of survival against the hard elements. To this day, humans require social interactions in order to develop healthy relationships, and it seems almost second nature for us to do so. From making friends at school to forming relationships with colleagues at work - when thrown into different environments, humans have a propensity for forging social bonds. In fact, humans as a species have formulated a whole new system to improve communication between our neighbours.

The rise of technology has enabled people to connect across greater distances more than ever before. What was once limited to small communities, contact via technology has enabled us to contact someone halfway across the globe in the blink of an eye, a feat that was barely possible 100 years ago. The internet allows people to video call one another, play games together, and connect with like-minded people where distance is the only obstacle. Social media can be used as a resource for various social and political movements as a medium to spread information and activism to promote positive change. Indeed, technology has changed human life and communication as we know it. However, the rise of technology has also introduced a digital culture that highlights only the best parts of life, a fallacy of what others' lives are like, and can actually lead people to feel more isolated. This isolation can cause people to seek out alternative avenues to satisfy the social niche that humans so very much need in order to stay healthy.

By 2021, more than half the people in the world (4.26 billion people) use social media, with the number expected to rise to 6 billion by 2027 (Dixon, 2022). Media is extremely accessible - you can access the internet from anywhere in the world that has an available signal, and with a phone on our person at all times, there are endless streams of content that we can indulge in due to the collective efforts of all users of the world wide web. It is no wonder that media addiction is so common. A survey read that more than 200 million people worldwide are estimated to suffer from addiction to social media and the internet (Maya, 2022). And this should be no surprise.

The internet was specifically made to keep user attention and to keep users invested and coming back to the corporations that supply them. Large companies use emotions as an active method of sales. Hollywood leverages user emotions when casting actors for movies, using beloved actors to get you to watch that hot new movie or dropping the nightmare actor so that it doesn't sully the movie's name. As stated before, talk show hosts will face a chair to the audience, so that the users feel more included in the program.

Now this may seem negative and manipulative, but having feelings of connections to particular media personnel is not inherently bad, nor is it new. As discussed before, the feeling of one-sided attachment to media figures, or parasocial relationships can be beneficial, especially when used in healthy ways. These emotions that a user has towards their subject or figure can feel like a true face-to-face interaction, and can satisfy the social niche that humans need, even though they are one-sided. As discussed before, parasocial interactions can bring a sense of comfort to users, and help them deal with unstableness in their lives. Social media and rises in technology in recent years have enabled us access to anyone and anything, endless people and characters to find ourselves in, to relate to, and to therefore find peace and comfort in. So what happens to the rate of parasocial relationships when the average person is faced with a global crisis that abruptly interrupts their ability to form and maintain regular in-person social contact, while also increasing time spent with screens? How do people use media to cope in a world that is increasingly more chaotic and uncertain?

The global COVID-19 pandemic of 2019 caused by the novel coronavirus, SARS-CoV-2 introduced a rare and unique opportunity to study the influence of social distancing on our relationships, both social and parasocial, as well as the connection between social isolation and elevated screen time during the lockdown (Bond, 2021).

COVID-19 is the name of a novel coronavirus that was first reported in December 2019. This particular virus and its subsequent variants cause fever, long-lasting cough and flu-like symptoms, and can range from mild symptoms where patients have to stay home to severe symptoms which require hospitalizations (Bazant and Bush, 2021). When COVID-19 was found to be transmitted through tiny droplets in the air, countries around the world required citizens to wear masks that covered their mouths and nose and implemented distancing measures, termed 'social distancing,' to prevent the spread of the virus (Bond, 2021). 'Social distancing' involved maintaining 6 feet of distance between each person and wearing facial coverings in public spaces, though there were not many public spaces accessible to the general population. Governments shut down schools and businesses alike, leaving only essential services like grocery stores open. Travel was halted, airports were shut down, and people were advised not to leave their houses, unless in the case of an emergency. This 'COVID-19 Lockdown' resulted in a massive decrease in face-to-face social interaction (Bond, 2021). At one point in Ontario, Canada, the government issued a 'COVID-19 social bubble' precaution, in which individuals could only interact with 5-10 people in their social circle, titled their 'social bubble' (Knope, 2020). Interaction with people outside of their social bubble could incur a fine. With schools and business closed, and social interaction limited to just 5 people, social interaction was at an all time low.

Luckily, the internet came to the rescue. Communication with others was achieved through online avenues - schools utilised videos and live streams to continue teaching classes, some even supplying students with laptops to complete their online homework on, while corporations would host webinars and meetings through video conferencing applications like Zoom and Microsoft Teams to continue business. During this time, people spent an unprecedented amount of time in front of their screens, and relied more heavily on technology than ever before. And not just for corporate work.

Individual leisure activities and streaming services skyrocketed during the pandemic (Dmitrieva and Tanzi, 2021). While some people picked up new hobbies like sewing or gardening, others turned to streaming services like Netflix, whose sales grew by a resounding 16 million subscriptions in the first three months of 2020, almost double that of its numbers in the final months of 2019 before the 'Stay-at-Home' orders were implemented (Thomas, 2020; Lee 2020). This easy accessibility towards media sources and an abrupt availability of free time led to a rise in screen time, which gave rise to more opportunities to form connections with favourite media personae and characters. But why do humans form these relationships when they are aware that they are one-sided, or even that they are forged with someone that does not even exist? What does participating in these relationships offer them?

We know that parasocial relationships can be used as comfort during uncertain times. The COVID-19 pandemic was an extraordinary scenario that most people had never seen in their lifetime, especially not one that played out on such a global scale. It is safe to say that times were quite uncertain - nobody knew what was going to happen and there was no similar situation to base our next steps on. As the outside world felt increasingly unsafe, fictional characters or controlled, one-sided online interactions were used as a source of stability and comfort (Hurwitz, 2022). When an individual engages in a parasocial relationship, they are primarily the creators of the interaction. People in parasocial relationships create the thoughts, dialogue, and scenario of the interaction, essentially projecting a personality onto a person who does not know they exist, or may not even exist themselves. Parasocial relationships are all about projection. Creating these personality features and projecting them onto a figure that in turn interacts with the user means that these relationships are more controlled than real-world relationships with others, and when analysed, usually provides users with a quality or feature they are looking for but cannot find in their own real-life face-to-face interactions (Hurwitz, 2022). In the case of the pandemic, a blooming time of uncertainty and instability, when social interaction was limited, it is no surprise that scientists found an increase in parasocial relationships, specifically in participants who experienced a decline in FtF interactions (Bond, 2021).

By collecting data via a series of questionnaires, scientists found that parasocial closeness growth was stronger among individuals who spent more time with their favourite media personae and less time communicating with friends FtF (Bond 2021).

Spending time with someone is crucial in developing relationships, and the same holds true for the development of a parasocial relationship with a fictional or media figure. And the pandemic offered the perfect environment for people to develop these dependencies. Let's look at the phases of developing a friendship and compare it to the conditions satisfied by the pandemic:

Many parasocial relationships involve figures that the user feels connected to in some way, in similar ways that youth and adults form face-to-face friendships with others who are similar to them. According to the article analysing the formation of friendship by iResearchnet.com, in real face-to-face relationships, individuals may find interactions with people who share a similar personality, behaviour style, or values easier than with individuals who are different from them. Therefore, they are more likely to engage in further interactions with similar people that can lead to the development and maintenance of a friendship (Friendship, 2017).

The maintenance of a friendship requires engaging in activities that serve to sustain the relationship. These actions may include sharing interests, doing activities together, and exchanging support and advice (Friendship, 2017). Similar activities are performed when an individual is involved in a parasocial relationship. In parasocial relationships, people describe using the figure as a friend to give them advice to help work out personal issues, much like a person would vent to a friend (O'Sullivan, 2021). Some describe using the figure to talk through problems that they feel they cannot speak out loud to other people in their life for fear of judgement. During the pandemic, people were faced with many issues - job layoffs, increased loneliness, the stress and anxiety as the virus hit closer and closer to home, which no doubt resulted in people increasingly confronting their projected figures rather than the (also stressed) people in their lives. Which leads to the second part of maintaining a relationship: frequency and convenience.

The frequency of interactions between friends is crucial in determining the success of a friendship. Frequency is described as the number of contacts or interactions that you have with another individual. The more you interact with someone whom you have positive experiences with, the stronger your relationship is expected to be. Convenience, or the ease of circumstances of which you are able to interact with someone, is an important determinant of how frequently you can interact with a friend (Friendship, 2017). Typically, maintaining a friendship is easier with individuals who are in close proximity with you than with those who are farther away, though again, the internet has made these long-distance interactions accessible at the push of a button. People can contact their friends through online platforms, at any time and from anywhere, making these online relationships easier to maintain. With the closure of leisure activities during the pandemic, many people were faced with increased free time. Indulging in media was an easy activity to partake in - it was convenient, and many frequently indulged in it whenever they had the chance, in order to distract themselves from their stuffy house confinement. With media-driven activities coupled with an increased loneliness and low social interactions, the development of parasocial relationships that people could access whenever they turned on their screens (which was often) can provide a gratifying feeling in an increasingly chaotic environment, therefore increasing the usage and need for that interaction. This can explain why scientists saw such an increase in parasocial relationships during this time period. The time during the COVID-19 pandemic truly was the perfect storm.

Conclusion

If there is one thing that is for certain, it is that humans have become heavily dependent on the internet and technological avenues for communication during the past 30 or so years, and after our heavy reliance on technology during the pandemic, this internet-focused trajectory does not seem to be slowing down. The internet played an important role in maintaining communication during a time of social isolation, and an even larger role in the development of parasocial relationships between media personnel and fans. These parasocial relationships greatly impacted people's mental health and provided individuals with a sense of stability, and an outlet to redirect their need for contact with other human beings. As technology continues to develop, it will be very interesting to see how humanity and the way we live, act, and communicate will evolve alongside it. The sky is truly the limit.

References

Bazant, M. Z., & Bush, J. W. (2021). A guideline to limit indoor airborne transmission of covid-19. Proceedings of the National Academy of Sciences, 118(17). https://doi.org/10.1073/pnas.2018995118.

Bond, B. J. (2021). Social and parasocial relationships during COVID-19 social distancing. Journal of Social and Personal Relationships, 38(8), 2308–2329. https://doi.org/10.1177/02654075211019129.

Dixon, S. (2022, June 15). Number of social media users 2025. Statista. Retrieved from https://www.statista.com/statistics/278414/number-of-worldwide-social-network-users/.

Dmitrieva, K., & Tanzi, A. (2021, July 23). More Lawn Care, Less Hair Care: Survey Shows U.S. Pandemic Habit. Bloomberg.com. Retrieved from https://www.bloomberg.com/news/articles/2021-07-23/what-did-americans-do-in-the-pandemic-here-s-how-they-answered.

Friendship. Psychology. (2017, March 16). Retrieved from http://psychology.iresearchnet.com/developmental-psychology/social-development/friendship/#:~:-text=The%20formation%20phase%20of%20a,bond%20that%20characterizes%20a%20friendship.

Hurwitz, S. (2022, February 18). Covid era sees uptick in use of parasocial relationships to self-soothe. Verywell Mind. Retrieved from https://www.verywell-mind.com/parasocial-relationships-covid-5218827.

Knope, J. (2020, September 29). Burst your social bubble and limit contact only to those in your household: Toronto's top doctor | CBC news. CBCnews. Retrieved from https://www.cbc.ca/news/canada/toronto/social-bubble-toronto-public-health-1.5742831.

Lee, W. (2020, April 21). Record high netflix subscriptions in Coronavirus Crisis. Los Angeles Times. Retrieved from https://www.latimes.com/entertainment-arts/business/story/2020-04-21/netflix-usage-profits-surge-during-coronavirus-crisis.

Maya. (2022, May 18). Social Media Addiction Statistics - TrueList 2022. TrueList. Retrieved from https://truelist.co/blog/social-media-addiction-statistics/.

O'Sullivan, S. (2021, October 4). The internet is obsessed with parasocial relationships. What Does Parasocial Relationship Mean? Retrieved from https://www.refinery29.com/en-ca/parasocial-relationships-online-cancelling-bon-appetit.

Thomas, Z. (2020, April 21). Netflix gets 16 million new sign-ups thanks to lockdown. BBC News. Retrieved from https://www.bbc.com/news/business-52376022.

Final Thoughts

By Madison Coutinho

Poem by Anjali Singh

Parasocial relationships are a one sided relationship that humans use for comfort to occupy their social niches. Evolutionarily, humans depend on social interactions to lead healthy and fulfilled lives, and engage in behaviours that mean to form bonds between family members and friends in order to do this. In contrast to the usual two-sided face-to-face relationships that we typically see, parasocial relationships serve to fill the same social niche that humans need without the required reciprocation from the other individual. This notion has been long present in history, and, when utilised correctly, can even be beneficial.

The capitalization of user emotions to support celebrity figures started as early as the 1920s, a decade or so after the emergence of the concept of "star." Currently, celebrity culture has evolved to reach even more emotional depth than before. With the emergence of technology, the range of avenues that aim to offer the means to form parasocial relationships has extended from mostly TV shows and black-and-white films, to any facet of entertainment available to the public. Parasocial relationships can be through figures seen in blogs, social media applications, video games and more, and with the help of the internet, can result in the creation of communities dedicated to speaking about and following a particular media personnel. These fan spaces, called fandoms, are a place where individuals who share similar interests can interact and bond over their chosen piece of media, often participating in creative activities such as creating fan-made content like fanfiction, videos, and animations. These spaces foster social identity and cohesion, as well as offer a sense of community and belonging, which are believed to positively affect health and well-being. Negative effects of being in fandom, like the doxxing and cyberbullying and tie this to mental health

We have previously spoken about the link between mental health and identity. The way an individual views themselves alters their definition of self-worth, and therefore, any external outlets that influence individuality, including social media, can have an impact on an individual's identity and the way they view themselves. Engaging in celebrity culture, a fallacy that highlights the positive and excludes the negative, can have detrimental effects on a young person's ideas of identity. When individuals select a celebrity in which they find appealing, they may wish to emulate the celebrity's features or qualities that they like. People who are perceived in this light can serve as role models, people to look up to, and formation of a strong identity.

On the flip side, it is important to keep in mind that celebrity culture often feeds the public lies. Celebrities are made to be perfectly polished and displayed for consumer eyes, and the perfect person that the user forms a parasocial relationship with, is often airbrushed to look that way.

It is crucial to recognize that parasocial relationships are the result of projecting illusions onto a figure that, though it may impersonate parts of a real-life relationship and offer a sense of intimacy and friendship, must to be recognized as false. Obsessive behaviours and celebrity worship can severely impact psychological integrity and health when a user cannot differentiate between fiction and reality. As our personal lives become more entangled with social media, this line between real and false becomes blurred, and it becomes difficult to discern what is authentic and what is posed to look as such.

Social media no doubt has had a large impact in the rate and ability in which people develop parasocial relationships. The internet has made celebrities and media personnel accessible anytime and anywhere. This dependence was made very prevalent when the world relied on the internet for school, business, and leisure during the COVID-19 pandemic. The rate of parasocial relationships increased during this time period, mostly as a result of increased time spent with media personnel, and decreases in social interaction with people in daily life. However, these parasocial bonds were pivotal in providing people with a sense of stability and comfort during a collective high stress period, and provided some emotional comfort during this time in their lives.

Parasocial relationships have been the subject of many a headline calling out crazy fan behaviour and the detrimental side effects of social media culture, though we have explored different reasons as to why parasocial relationships are not just normal, but can be beneficial when used correctly. Though a one-sided fictitious relationship may seem peculiar, when you consider the underlying meaning of why they exist, when you look behind the curtain at what parasocial relationships signify - the most biological need for human closeness- we can begin to unravel what it means to form relationships with others, and what it means to truly be human.

A secret admirer: A character from the play, an impersonator from the audience. It may be the static side-character, but they find pleasure simply being in the play. Someone who is silent and remains unseen.

Someone who is patient yet despised, loved and everything in between.
Your eyes fix on one thing, one person.Your ears hear only their name.
Admiration, even love, is fine, but it may not be wise to cross that line.
The fan is to influencer as the moon is to a star. A relationship that dates
:back decades.

The celebrity you worship, the fandom that is your masquerade,
There's someone that has you saying, "I love you, until the end of time, but there is
a cost to this seemingly innocent crime"

Lightning Source UK Ltd.
Milton Keynes UK
UKHW011109060223
416538UK00001B/155

9 781773 698533